# THE
# CHINESE
# WORLD

# THE CHINESE WORLD

Richard Yang
Edward J. Lazzerini

FORUM PRESS

# THE WORLD OF ASIA SERIES

WILLIAM J. MILLER, Consulting Editor

## THE CHINESE WORLD

**RICHARD YANG**
Washington University

**EDWARD J. LAZZERINI**
University of New Orleans

## THE INDIAN WORLD

**C. JAMES BISHOP**
Manchester College

**DAVID KOPF**
University of Minnesota

## THE SOUTHEAST ASIAN WORLD

**JOHN F. CADY**
Ohio University

## THE JAPANESE WORLD

**WILLIAM J. MILLER**
St. Louis University

Published simultaneously in Canada.

Printed in the United States of America.

Library of Congress Catalog Card Number: 77-81184

ISBN: 0-88273-504-7

Cover design by Mike Whitney and Barbara Hueting

# Contents

# *Preface*

Chinese civilization is not the world's oldest, having been preceded in birth by those that emerged in the valleys of the Tigris-Euphrates and Indus Rivers to the west. Yet, beginning with the development of their earliest urban culture around 1600 B.C., the Chinese had until 1949 maintained a civilization whose character survived longer than any other. This fact contributed to a striking continuity in their lives over the centuries. Continuity, however, does not mean unchanging, static, or any of the other terms used popularly to describe China before the twentieth century. For most of their history the Chinese people have nurtured a culture as evolutionary as most and have time and time again shown themselves to possess more than their share of human genius, vitality, and inventiveness.

We have, in this concise volume, surveyed without oversimplification the history of China from its shrouded beginnings down through the deaths of Chiang Kai-shek, Mao Tse-tung and the early post-Mao political turmoil. It was necessary to include only the most significant developments and trends in Chinese history in the interest of brevity. Nevertheless, we have endeavored as much as possible to provide the non-expert, whether student, traveler, or simply interested reader, with more than merely a compilation of details by including frequent analyses of the Chinese story.

A modern Chinese scholar observed, "Most of the time, foreigners know us better than we know ourselves." He may have been too kind to most Westerners, especially Americans, who have long labored under the burden of changing myths about China. THE CHINESE WORLD should help to dispel some of the lingering misconceptions about China's distant and more recent past, without creating new ones.

We appreciate the assistance of Dr. Rita Adams of Saint Louis University and Miss Rita Kwapiszeski in typing the manuscripts of THE

CHINESE WORLD as well as the other volumes in THE WORLD OF ASIA project. A special mention is made of Annie W. Yang and Sue-Dee Lazzerini, who greatly assisted with their advice and help in lightening the task of manuscript preparation.

In addition, we wish to thank Dr. John Vogt, who prepared the maps for this and the other volumes in the series, to William J. Miller, Consulting Editor of the series, whose suggestions and direction have been invaluable, to Irene E. Miller, Forum Press Editor, and to Erby M. Young, Managing Director of Forum Press, who conceived THE WORLD OF ASIA Series.

# Introduction

CHINA TODAY, with perhaps 900,000,000 people, is the world's most populated nation. In fact, one out of every four persons at present speaks some dialect of Chinese. Stretching over 3.7 million square miles — from the Amur River in the north to Southeast Asia and the South China Sea, and from the Pamir Mountains in the west to the Pacific Ocean in the east — China ranks third behind the Soviet Union and Canada in area. Only somewhat larger than the United States and lying within that country's approximate latitudes, she experiences much the same climatic range and variety.

Despite being endowed with a topography that has historically encouraged regional separatism, China owes much to geographic factors for her remarkable cultural unity. The country's location at one extremity of Eurasia and the existence of formidable natural barriers (mountains, deserts, wastelands, and oceans) along her periphery have traditionally isolated her from the rest of the world and militated against extensive contacts with the other great centers of civilization. Such geographic isolation, confining though it may have been, has nevertheless stimulated the Chinese to cultivate a rich and, for the most part, indigenous culture that has never lost contact with its point of origin.

The country comprises two general areas: China Proper (the historic homeland of the Chinese) and the outlying territories of Manchuria, Mongolia, Sinkiang, and Tibet (all situated along China's frontiers and never settled by significant numbers of Chinese). China Proper has three main divisions, each centered in a river valley. In the north the Yellow River flows for 2,700 miles through an area often called "brown China." Because of irregular rainfall, this semi-arid region yields only one crop a year (usually wheat, millet, or soy beans) from its wind-blown loess soil. Frequent flooding by the Yellow River has enriched the land but has often caused great destruction. Rightfully it has earned the epithet "China's

Sorrow." Farther south, the Yangtze, China's longest river (3,100 miles), dominates a second area of China Proper. Called "green China," this region enjoys forty inches of rainfall a year and produces tea, rice, and silk. The lower Yangtze valley became in time the population center and heart of the country. Her largest city, Shanghai, lies near the river's mouth. Finally, the mountainous south and the adjacent West River valley make up the third area of China Proper, which for some time also included the Tonkin Delta of northern Vietnam. Canton, China's second largest port city, overlooks the mouth of the West River. This area became the country's greatest rice-growing region.

Manchuria, the richest of the four outlying territories of China, lies to the north of the capital city of Peking beyond the Great Wall. The region produces timber and wheat on its fertile plains, as well as some coal and iron. To the west of Manchuria is Mongolia, a land of desert and grassy steppe and the home of nomads who often invaded the Yellow River valley. Beyond Mongolia, in distant Central Asia, one finds Sinkiang, an area of high mountains and deserts, through which pass the only significant overland routes leading westward. Tibet lies adjacent to the forbidding Himalayas (bordering India to the south) and is a land whose remoteness, intense cold, and aridity have proved enormous obstacles to economic development.

# 1

# Formative Age to the Later Empire (Prehistory-1800)

THE EARLIEST EVIDENCE of settled life in China dates from around 4000 B.C. in the area of the northern bend of the Yellow River. From that time until the beginning of the second millennium B.C., the process leading to the birth of Chinese civilization developed slowly. While archaeologists have striven to understand precisely what took place during the late prehistoric period, the Chinese have long possessed a mythical explanation for the origins of their first societies. It rests upon the unsubstantiated claim that civilized life was taught them by a number of "culture heroes" who showed them how to farm and domesticate animals, instituted family life, created a rudimentary central government, and introduced the bow and arrow, the calendar, silk cloth, ceramics, and above all, writing. The last of these "culture heroes," named Yü, is supposed to have built dams for flood control and established China's first recorded dynasty, the Hsia, around 2205 B.C. The dynasty may indeed have been legendary, yet its place in Chinese mythology is strong indication that the tradition of unified government has roots deep in China's past.

Chinese recorded history begins about 1766 B.C., when a fierce tribe of Mongolian stock, brandishing weapons of bronze, conquered the central portion of the Yellow River area and established the Shang dynasty. Excavations in the region have verified the existence of such a dynasty and the society which it ruled. However, as with all ancient peoples, our knowledge of Shang China is sketchy indeed. We do know that the Shang cultivated both wheat and millet and may have introduced also a system of irrigation for growing rice. Furthermore, it would appear that they ate dog flesh and pork and domesticated the goat, sheep, ox, horse, and chicken. Although pit dwellers at first, the Shang eventually built houses set on foundations of the closely packed loess soil of the region, with thatched roofs raised by wooden walls.

Two of the more intriguing features of Shang culture were its mastery of advanced techniques of working bronze and its development of writing. While bronze was used for a wide range of products, the most extraordinary pieces included drinking cups, chalices, libation bowls, and vases or urns of diverse sizes and shapes whose purposes may have been largely religious or ceremonial. Since the form of many Shang bronze vessels was obviously derived from the pottery styles of earlier cultures in the area, scholars have been at a loss to explain their astonishingly high level of artistry and technique in the absence of evidence of a more primitive local bronze technology. This has fueled speculation that a considerable influence from the Near East may have contributed to this Shang phenomenon.

Even more significant are the written records that have come down to us from the Shang period. Composed on animal bone, horn, or tortoise shells, numerous incriptions have survived to provide us with the oldest known form of Chinese writing and most of our knowledge of Shang history. They utilized these bones for divination, with the inscriptions addressed to deities or to deceased relatives often on matters of family concern — the origins of Chinese ancestor veneration. As for the script, specialists have determined that the basic features and principles which characterize the present-day Chinese writing system developed in Shang times.

In addition, the Shang were consummate warriors. They effectively walled in their chief settlements and took advantage of a superiority in military hardware provided by horse-drawn chariots to subdue their neighbors. Prisoners-of-war provided a major source of slaves and also hapless victims for the human sacrifices performed in their religious ceremonials.

## • The Age of Feudalism

Around the year 1122 B.C., a western tribe subject to the Shang, the Chou, defeated the forces of its overlord and established a new dynasty in China. The Chou leadership took much from the Shang elite, especially its writing system, and intermarried with it in order to consolidate the new administration. Declaring that the last Shang ruler had been guilty of terrible crimes — and hence had forfeited the right to govern — the Chou sought to legitimize their power by claiming that they had come to the throne by means of the rebellious actions of the people and with the "Mandate of Heaven" (*T'ien-ming*). In so doing, the new dynasts introduced the concept that the people have a right granted by Heaven to challenge a corrupt and unjust ruler. As the Chou proclaimed: "Heaven sees and hears through the eyes and ears of the people." Therefore, the new leaders assumed the title "Son of Heaven" (*T'ien-tzu*). This political idea has justified virtually every dynastic change in China since that time.

Historians divide the Chou period of Chinese history into two principal eras: Western Chou (from ca. 1122-771 B.C.), with the capital located at Hao, and Eastern Chou (771-256 B.C.), during which the royal family and court resided in Loyang. Throughout most of the first period, the Chou managed generally to maintain order in North China and to expand the frontiers of their realm. But even then, owing to the practice of decentralizing authority by allowing members of the royal family, favorites, and even descendants of the former Shang elite to exercise autonomy in parceled-out regions, the Chou experienced difficulty in preserving the unity of their state. As time went on the kings were less and less successful in commanding the loyalty of subordinates as the latter slowly began to identify their own interests more with their allotted territories than with the central government. According to historian Charles O. Hucker, by the time the Chou were forced to transfer their capital in order to escape the threat of barbarian attack, the foundation of a feudal society (with fiefs, vassalage, and proto-contractual arrangements) was already in place.

After the move to Loyang, the central government ceased to wield any real power. Instead, the various regional states that emerged in increasing numbers like the cells of a beehive exercised whatever authority there was in China. Some of the local lords even presumed during the later stages of the period to call themselves "king" (*wang*), a title previously reserved for the Chou ruler. And so it went for some four hundred years more, with the Chou powerless to reign with authority and no single lord strong enough to win out over all others. At first, conflicts among the various states were more diplomatic than military, a matter of adroit maneuvering rather than actual fighting. But by the fifth century B.C., a change had come over those who now participated in Chinese politics: inter-state conflict became a deadly affair. As war intensified, only the strong could survive, and with time the number of independent states decreased. Driven by the ambition to capture the Mandate by military action, each of the lords exhausted himself in the protracted struggle. The ensuing chaos and destruction finally ended in the third century B.C., when the western kingdom of Ch'in overran the other states. Not surprisingly, however, all the rapid and confusing change had called forth a marvelous effort by thinking Chinese to re-examine the traditions and institutions of their society and to seek a path to a more normal and harmonious existence in a new and unprecedented era of Chinese intellectualism.

## • Life in Chou Times

Before turning to a discussion of the intellectual ferment of the later Chou period, it might be well to survey some of the other developments down to the third century B.C. which contributed to the formation of so much of what we identify as traditionally Chinese.

In the realm of politics and administrative practice we have already noted the concept of the Mandate of Heaven, but to this we must add a number of other principles which became firmly established: that a single ruler (the Son of Heaven) should reign with effective centralized control over all of China; that to govern well a ruler must heed the advice of his counselors and officials; that the government had the right and obligation to exert its authority in all areas of life; and that it should show a genuine concern for the welfare of the people. Beyond these principles, the political leaders of the Chou period took steps to improve and rationalize their administrations by instituting regular taxation and substituting appointive offices for hereditary ones.

The Chou era also witnessed the rooting of two fundamental features of Chinese social organization: the family and class differentiation. The family had served as China's basic social unit at least since Shang times, but with the growth of population, the clan, based on blood kinship, extended the family's significance and added a new dimension to the country's social development that has persisted to this day. At the same time, the Chinese were proceeding to develop a society in which class distinctions were paramount. The traditional division into five classes — scholar-officials, peasants, artisans, merchants, and soldiers, ranked in that order — rested on several criteria, but the most important was occupation. To the Chinese, some occupations (those demanding intellectual rather than manual labor, for example) made greater contributions to society and were therefore more important and more worthy than others.

Finally, important developments occurred in Chinese economic activity. The use of money, largely copper coins, expanded particularly for interregional trade. New implements such as the hoe and ox-drawn plow were introduced into agriculture, as was the so-called "well-field system" of land distribution, whereby eight families lived on a central plot (with a well), worked it in communal fashion for the local lord, and labored individually on one of eight surrounding plots for their own welfare. Despite the difficulty of maintaining this system in hard times and against land speculators, it became the traditional, ideal method of Chinese landholding.

## ● The "Hundred Schools of Thought:" Confucianism

Amidst the social and political chaos of the later Chou period, a small group of men, mostly from aristocratic families, began to devote themselves to study and contemplation. Out of their dissatisfaction with contemporary Chinese life emerged such broad and sophisticated criticism of the established conventions and institutions that the parameters of Chinese philosophy were essentially defined for all but the most recent periods of Chinese history. The analyses of and prescriptions for current ills were numerous enough for later Chinese to talk of this philosophical flowering as the "Hundred Schools of Thought." Of the various "schools" five proved to have the most lasting significance for Chinese culture: Confucianism, Taoism, Moism, Naturalism, and Legalism.

In its essential points, the first was the intellectual product of Confucius, or K'ung Fu-tzu (Master K'ung), who was born in 551 B.C. to a lower-ranking, possibly impoverished aristocratic family. Information concerning his life is sketchy and of doubtful authenticity, but we are reasonably sure that his early years were spent in difficult and humble circumstances. Except for about a decade in mid-life when he wandered about North China trying to convince the region's rulers to apply his principles, Confucius devoted his mature years to teaching.

Confucius viewed politics as an ethical problem and social improvement as a matter of individual morality. Order and good government would return to society only when the ruler and his administrators reformed themselves and set moral standards for the rest of the population. As grass bends with the wind, to paraphrase a Confucian aphorism, so society is influenced by the ruler. Because Confucius believed that knowledge led to virtue, he emphasized the major role that education should play to ensure proper leadership.

Fang Lei vessel of cast bronze. Early Western Chou (1122-771 B.C.). The Saint Louis Art Museum.

The great sage also upheld what the Chinese call *jen*, a virtue which encompasses benevolence, love, compassion, and sympathy toward one's fellow man. The stress on *jen* reveals the central humanism (or man-centered orientation) of his philosophy. Cultivation of this virtue creates the "gentleman" (*chün-tzu*), the person who is "as concerned about what is right as the petty man is about what is profitable." Anyone, regardless of birth or wealth, could aspire to the perfection that was the *chün-tzu*'s, and achievement of it should be most highly honored. Because such ideals challenged the established aristocratic order, some historians have regarded Confucius as an anti-feudal revolutionary.

There is, however, another side to Confucianism which is explicitly conservative. He proclaimed the writings of the ancients to be the most important guides to virtuous behavior and extolled the Duke of Chou (twelfth-eleventh century B.C.) as the ideal ruler. Likewise, he taught respect for authority and deference to superiors as expressed in the term *li* (social and moral propriety) and in the five basic human relationships: ruler to subject, father to son, elder brother to younger brother, husband to wife, and friend to friend, the first four of which were relationships between superiors and inferiors. These also stressed the eminence of the family, the fundamental social unit for Confucius. He clearly viewed himself not as an innovator, but merely as a transmitter of the old ways.

Throughout the *Analects*, that collection of pithy Confucian "sayings," which provides us with our single reliable source for his thought, we find the sage attempting to deal with the everyday world of social problems and individual relationships. There is a noticeable lack of interest in religion and theology except in a negative sense, as when he says "Being unable yet to serve men, how can one serve the spirits," or "Not yet understanding life, how can one understand death?" Instead, Confucius emphasized that it is better for man to focus his attention on immediate human problems. Leave the spirits to themselves.

One of Confucius's most important disciples was Mencius (ca. 372-289 B.C.), sometimes called the "Saint Paul of Confucianism." Like his mentor, Mencius emphasized the equation between knowledge and virtue, especially for the ruler, who should cultivate "sageliness within and kingliness without." More significantly, he stressed that the virtue of a ruler must be measured by his benevolence to his people. Thus the first duty of a government was to ensure the material well-being of the population; failure to do so provided grounds for popular rebellion. If successful, the revolt would clearly signify the withdrawal of the Mandate of Heaven.

While historians regard Mencius as a sentimentalist and idealist, they tend to see Hsün Tzu (ca. 300-235 B.C.), another Confucian of great stature, as a harsh, unsentimental rationalist. Unlike Mencius, whose humanistic emphasis rested on the belief that man was by nature good, Hsün Tzu regarded human nature as innately evil. He certainly acknowledged that education could correct personal faults and lead to virtue, but he also insisted that law, coercion, and discipline were required to control man's natural inclination to wickedness. While this last point bore some resemblance to the basic argument of the Legalists, it would be unfair and misleading to draw the parallel too closely. Hsün Tzu, despite his assessment of man's basic character, remained a humanist.

Over the centuries the basic doctrines of Confucius would be reinterpreted time and again by his followers. Through it all, however,

Confucianism survived because of its practicality devoid of mysticism, its humanity, its simplicity, and its appeal to the nobler instincts in man through reverence for virtue, respect for learning, and devotion to family.

## • The "Hundred Schools of Thought:" Taoism

Obscurity clouds the roots of Taoism even more than those of Confucianism. One tradition holds that a certain Lao Tzu (Old Master) served for many years as keeper of the imperial archives at Loyang before giving up his post to head west into Central Asia. Along the way, as he passed through the Great Wall, the gatekeeper admonished him by saying: "Old Man, you have lived a long time and know a great deal. Why don't you write it down before you die?" In response Lao Tzu composed the 5,000-character text of the *Tao-te Ching* (Classic of the Way and of Virtue) and thereby provided the basic source of Taoist teaching.

In opposition to the humanistic thrust of Confucianism, Taoism emphasized nature and man's harmony with it. Whereas Confucius advocated the pursuit of knowledge to attain virtue and hence the path (*Tao*) to happiness, the philosophy of Lao Tzu suggested something quite different: relaxed conformity to nature. Because civilization had corrupted man and forced him to act contrary to nature, he should withdraw from society with its formalities and ceremonials and fit himself into the great natural pattern. To oppose nature could only bring misery to man.

The ideal society for the Taoists had existed in primitive times before men needed conventions; by the same token the unborn child represented the perfect man. As the way to happiness, the Tao defies precise definition; it is "nameless," "formless," and "fathomless." The individual must accommodate himself to the impersonal natural order, actually realizing and attaining everything by doing nothing. As water overcomes obstacles in its path by flowing around them, so the *Tao* triumphs by adjusting and yielding. Thus, while the Confucians had urged the ruler to direct society by moral example, the Taoists preferred that authority be discreet, governing without appearing to govern.

Although in most ways contradictory, Confucianism and Taoism complemented each other in molding the Chinese mind. Like two great rivers, they flowed through Chinese philosophy, art, and literature, appealing simultaneously to opposite sides of the Chinese character. While Confucianism taught the Chinese to be sober, moralistic, and hard-working, Taoism urged them to relax, enjoy life a little more, and cultivate their individuality. In both philosophies the Chinese found principles of enormous value that served some part of their social and personal needs. As a popular saying suggested: When in power an official followed Confucianism, but after leaving office he preferred the tranquility which Taoism offered.

## • The "Hundred Schools of Thought:" Moism, Naturalism, and Legalism

Mo Tzu (ca. 470-391 B.C.) seems to have begun his intellectual odyssey as a Confucianist but to have ended it by formulating a philosophy that directly challenged revered tenets of Confucianism. For example, he regarded Confucian concern for ritual and ceremony as not only foolish and worthless but also wasteful. Man should devote his attention to what is useful in promoting the material welfare of society; in fact, happiness for Mo Tzu more than for any of the other leading philosophers was defined in material terms.

In addition to his materialism and utilitarianism, Mo Tzu is noted for his emphasis on religion (being the only important philosopher to view religion as a means to promote proper human behavior), his concern for the middle and lower classes, and his demand for "universal love," which included a call for the abandonment of war. The latter proved especially disturbing to Confucianists, because in advocating the idea of "love for all men equally," he scorned the family's place of honor.

Although Mo Tzu presented his philosophy in a more systematic and logical manner than did most of the other sages, it proved impossible to implement. As a result, despite affirming some rather profound truths, his writings received little attention in later centuries.

For its part, the Naturalist school taught that two balancing cosmic forces — the *yin* (female, passive, cold, and dark) and the *yang* (male, active, warm, and light) — governed reality. This pair, later complemented by the "five agents" theory, which argued that wood, metal, fire, water, and earth determined all natural events, represented the endless alternation of opposites throughout all nature. The symbol of this mode of thinking was a disc divided into two equal parts by a curved line, with each part shaded differently yet containing a spot of the other's color to illustrate their distinction as well as their harmonious interplay. Although Naturalism failed to develop into a true school of thought, its concepts influenced later Chinese views concerning the physical universe and probably encouraged the Chinese proclivity to synthesize diverse philosophies.

The last of the "hundred schools," Legalism, belongs in the same category as Confucianism and Taoism in terms of importance for the development of Chinese culture. Yet it stands out from these two schools by its emphasis on law, its single-minded concern for the prosperity and survival of the state, its negative attitude toward human nature and the latter's potential for improvement, and its cynicism and amorality. The Legalists found both the Confucian emphasis on *li* and the Taoist encouragement of "non-action" to be impractical and ineffectual as means for ensuring good government. Instead they argued for a system of elaborately defined laws and regulations, replete with explicit, even exaggerated rewards and punishments, in order to compel men to be good. A regimented population ruled over by an authoritarian monarch was the ideal for which the Legalists strove. In the Machiavellian tradition, what mattered to them in the final analysis was power, not virtue, wisdom, or talent as proclaimed by others.

Out of the era of the late Chou dynasty there thus emerged a number of contending philosophies providing analyses of China's problems and visions of her future. Despite the success of several of them in dominating Chinese culture at different times, that domination was never complete. Except for the brief period of the Ch'in dynasty discussed below, the Chinese never chose one philosophy to the exclusion of the others, but rather tended to accept principles from at least the five treated here in order to create a philosophical synthesis. In the long run eclecticism rather than exclusivity came to characterize the intellectual underpinnings of Chinese society and culture.

## • China Unified: The Ch'in Dynasty (221-207 B.C.)

Ch'in emerged as a small state located in a valley of the Wei River west of the Chou domain. Constantly threatened by barbarian attacks, the Ch'in rulers gradually organized their state along authoritarian, military lines, subordinating everything and everyone to the will of the monarch. Shang Yang, a fourth-century B.C. prime minister and one of the initial practitioners of Legalism, built perhaps the first totalitarian state in history. His policies, which included organized forced labor, military training, and secret police surveillance, fully regimented Ch'in society. To ensure law and order, the state held people responsible not only for their own acts but for those of relatives as well. As a political tactic, the Ch'in condoned any action that might prove beneficial to the state, including assassination and deception. For example, when Shang Yang arranged a conference with a neighboring ruler in order to discuss a border dispute, the prime minister ambushed him, scattering his army and seizing his territory.

A well-prepared Ch'in campaign led to the conquest of the Chou in 256 B.C. Within the ensuing thirty years six more states were overrun as easily "as a silkworm devours a mulberry leaf." Northern and central China fell under Ch'in domination by 221 B.C., and with the completion of military action the new rulers of China launched policies designed to obliterate the feudal system and unify the country.

King Cheng, who proclaimed himself "First Emperor" (Shih Huang-ti), successfully completed this task. He extended the central administration of the Ch'in to the whole country, abolished the old feudal states, divided the now unified empire into administrative districts and sub-districts, and brought an end to nepotism in government employment. To contribute further to the unification of China, the First Emperor standardized the laws, customs, written language, weights and measures, agricultural tools, and even the length of cart axles so that their wheels would fit set grooves in the roadways. He also inaugurated tremendous public works projects to improve and expand China's irrigation system and construct highways (often two hundred and fifty feet wide) to link various parts of the country. Perhaps his most famous and impressive project was the construction of a fifteen-hundred-mile fortified wall to protect China's northeastern frontier from invading barbarians. Known as the Great Wall, this structure averages twenty-five feet in elevation with towers from thirty-five to forty feet high situated every two hundred to three hundred yards. Its width of twenty-five feet at the base tapers to about fifteen feet at the top — wide enough for four horsemen to ride or eight soldiers to walk abreast. Like some enormous grey serpent, the wall follows a winding course over mountains and valleys equal to the distance from New York City to Omaha.

To accompany his other policies and projects, the First Emperor took concrete steps to ensure intellectual uniformity and suppress dissent by banning philosophical debate, prohibiting glorification of the past or criticism of the present, and proscribing all writings other than official Ch'in chronicles and practical manuals relating to agriculture, medicine, or divination. Since no one was allowed to possess any other texts, all copies were ordered collected and burned except for those that would be preserved in the imperial library for use by government officials.

Although the emperor boasted of establishing a dynasty on Legalistic principles which would endure for "ten thousand generations," his oppressive policies inspired only terror and enmity in the hearts of his

The Great Wall of China dates from the third century B.C. It extends for 1,500 miles from the coast to the frontier of Outer Mongolia. Wide World Photos.

subjects. When the inevitable revolt began in 207 B.C., the Ch'in quickly lost all popular support. A new leader, Liu Pang, emerged from the ranks of the peasantry to overthrow the dynasty and claim the Mandate of Heaven which the Ch'in had forfeited. Though ruling only briefly, the Ch'in, nevertheless, bequeathed to China their family name and a de-feudalized political system which, despite later events, would remain features of Chinese life until the end of the imperial system in 1911-1912.

## • The Han and the Institutionalization of Confucianism (202 B.C.-220 A.D.)

Emerging from the chaos which followed the collapse of the Ch'in, a new dynasty calling itself Han assumed power in 202 B.C. and proceeded to build a new state. Because Ch'in harshness and brutality had caused their overthrow, the Han carefully avoided imitating the extreme methods of their predecessors. To despise Ch'in excesses, however, did not mean abandoning those institutions and practices which had proved so successful in unifying the country and re-establishing order and centralized government. Some aspects of Legalism may have been distasteful to the new regime (the early leaders of which were inclined more toward Taoism), but there was no denying that as far as the daily practice of politics was concerned, Legalism more than any of the other major philosophies seemed more realistic.

On the one hand, then, the organizational structure and administrative practices of the new regime remained rooted in Legalistic thinking. Not long after taking power, however, the Han leadership realized that Legalism could not by itself, unless implemented in the Ch'in manner, be the ideological basis of society. As a result, the government very quickly invited Confucian scholars into official service. After that, Confucianism (not unaffected by the other major schools of thought) gradually rose to such prominence that it was finally declared the state ideology in 124 B.C. With the introduction of a Confucian curriculum into the national university founded in that same year and with the somewhat later (6 A.D.) establishment of a competitive civil service examination system based on Confucian writings, the Confucianization of Chinese culture and politics was well under way.

The Han dynasty reigned continually for a little over four hundred years except for a brief period between 9 and 23 A.D., when Wang Mang, the highly popular chief minister, usurped the throne. As emperor, Wang proclaimed a new dynasty (Hsin), but even more importantly inaugurated a series of reforms that if fully implemented would have revolutionized Chinese society. By the time of Wang's rule, much of the general prosperity of the earlier Han period had waned, because of a large increase in the peasant population and the appropriation of more and more land by the small elite class. Together the two phenomena had the effect not only of creating within the peasant class a substantial number of landless families, but also of reducing tax revenues for the state. In order to reverse these trends, Wang Mang proposed a program that included the nationalization of all land, its equitable redistribution, price fixing, government loans to poor farmers at low interest rates, and the abolition of slavery.

The written records do not reveal clearly the reasons for the failure of Wang's reforms. Right from the beginning all sorts of natural disasters and freakish events cast an ominous shadow over his reign and may have diminished the popularity he had once enjoyed. Possibly certain groups in society, particularly the wealthy landowners who stood to lose the most by the proposed changes, obstructed his efforts. In any event, Wang's reform program barely got underway before it began to experience difficulties. The outbreak of rebellion sparked by drought, famine, and numerous breakdowns of the diking system, coupled with declining support from the great families of China, led to Wang's death and the end of his short-lived dynasty. After some further conflict among the various pretenders to the throne, the future Emperor Kuang-wu defeated his rivals and proclaimed the restoration of the Han dynasty in 25 A.D.

The four centuries of Han rule are noteworthy for major developments in literature. First, along with the recognition of Confucianism as the official state ideology, a number of texts transmitted from pre-Ch'in times were thought to embody truths of such significance that they came to be esteemed as the *Five Classics*. These texts of often-disputed date and authorship included the *I-ching* (Classic of Changes), the *Shu-ching* (Classic of Writings), the *Shih-ching* (Classic of Songs), the *Ch'un-ch'iu* (Spring and Autumn Annals), and the *Li-ching* (Classic of Rituals). Together the five were regarded as essential for the maintenance of Chinese civilization and along with later additions to the list served as the sources upon which the government based the civil service examinations.

Second, historiography, stimulated by the invention of paper, experienced an upsurge of activity that produced two impressive achievements. One was the *Shih-chi* (Records of the Historian), begun by Ssu-ma T'an (d. 110 B.C.) and completed by his son Ssu-ma Ch'ien (145-87 B.C.?). Although this work is largely a compilation of excerpts from original sources, it is more than a mere chronicle. In it the authors explore the interrelationships among events, display a keen interest in the personalities of important people, and show an awareness of the changing nature of institutions and social practices over time. The second major historical writing was the *Han-shu* (Book of Han) by Pan Ku (32-92 A.D.). The author imitated Ssu-ma Ch'ien in his organization of the *Han-shu*, but he surpassed his predecessor by introducing several new subjects into his text, including a bibliography and sections on justice and administrative geography.

Before leaving the Han we should mention that the dynasty fulfilled the concept of China as the "Middle Kingdom" (or *Chung-kuo* — "right in the middle" — China as the center of the universe) by pacifying the barbarian tribes on all its frontiers. Imperial forces defeated the Hsiung-nu (Huns) in the north and extended dominion in the south into coastal Annam and Tonkin, present-day Vietnam. Late in the dynasty's history, the Han imperium reached westward to the Caspian Sea and, in so doing, activated trade with Europe via Sinkiang and Central Asia along what became known as the "silk route."

## • The Era of Disunity (220-581 A.D.) and the Advent of Buddhism

The Empire of the Han disintegrated in the early third century A.D. in ways comparable to the experience of Rome in a slightly later period. In both instances, causal factors included an imbalance of wealth, a decline of loyalty to the empire, and a shortage of arable land. When the end came, fragmentation and decentralization were some of the immediate results; in China several kingdoms made their appearance, none particularly significant. At the same time internal division invited barbarian incursions across China's northern frontiers into the Yellow River valley, but the Chinese managed to hold at the line of the Yangtze. At this time, however, the center of Chinese culture began a move to the south that would be completed centuries later.

The ensuing era of political disunity, which saw northern China controlled by various nomadic groups of non-Chinese, continued until 581, when a northern dynasty, Sui, reunified the country and restored effective central government. In times of crisis like the third through sixth centuries A.D., people frequently seek the consolation of religion. Just as Christianity penetrated the Roman Empire in her period of collapse, so Buddhism gained prominence in the era of disunity that followed the Han. This religion first arrived in China about 1 A.D., and by 65 A.D. the country already had a Buddhist community. Only in the fourth century, however, did this alien faith begin its dynamic growth on Chinese soil.

The basic tenets of Buddhism are contained in the Four Noble Truths: (1) All life is suffering; (2) Suffering originates in desire; (3) Suffering can be escaped only by a complete suppression of desire; and (4) Desire can be overcome only by following the Noble Eight-Fold Path consisting of right views, right intentions, right speech, right conduct, right livelihood, right effort, right mindfulness, and right concentration. Success in conquering desire leads to the attainment of Nirvana, a state of perfect peace and bliss. In a sense, then, Buddhism offered to the Chinese a promise of an afterlife hitherto lacking in their philosophies and religions.

In many respects Buddhism challenged basic Chinese beliefs and attitudes. For example, monastic celibacy contradicted the Chinese respect for family life and the whole notion of filial piety; asceticism ran counter to Chinese humanism; while mendicancy collided with the Chinese disdain for beggars. Yet its spiritual qualities attracted many discouraged people previously more concerned with the worldliness of Confucianism. (For much the same reason Taoism enjoyed a resurgence of popularity during this same period.) In keeping with the Chinese habit of intellectual syncretism and tolerance of diverse views — and despite two serious official efforts to repress the religion — Buddhism soon found a permanent place in Chinese culture.

## • The Restoration of Political Unity and the T'ang (581-906 A.D.)

Despite the collapse of the Han dynasty and with it all remnants of central administration in China, the idea of empire survived (particularly in the south) to be resuscitated in the late sixth century by a barbarian, but Sinicized, northern state, the Sui. The effort to reunite the country, however, so exhausted the new dynasty that it was unable to retain the throne for more than a generation. Like the Ch'in before it, though, the Sui prepared the way for the establishment of a much more powerful and long-lived dynasty, the T'ang (618-906 A.D.), which led China to new heights of cultural, economic, military, and administrative achievements.

The T'ang extended the empire's frontiers to their greatest limits yet attained. Campaigns led to the inclusion of Korea, parts of Manchuria, Tonkin, and the areas of present-day Sinkiang and Tibet under China's sway as imperial armies everywhere subdued barbarian neighbors and forced them to acknowledge the Chinese emperor as their overlord. The pattern of diplomatic relations that developed between these peoples and China became an institution known as the tributary system. Originated by the Han, this system allowed foreign peoples to retain their native leaders yet secure Chinese protection in return for periodic tribute in the form of native products (largely symbolic) and homage rendered to the emperor in the imperial capital in recognition of the superiority of the ruler of the Middle Kingdom.

Owing to the expansion of international trade, stimulated in large part by a world-wide demand for silk and Chinese porcelain, foreign cultures in the T'ang era affected Chinese life to a greater degree than in any previous dynasty. Contacts with the West were renewed, and trading ships from India and Arabia exchanged wares at southern Chinese ports, bringing tea from Southeast Asia for the first time. The impact of foreign religions deepened during these centuries. Indian Buddhist priests and

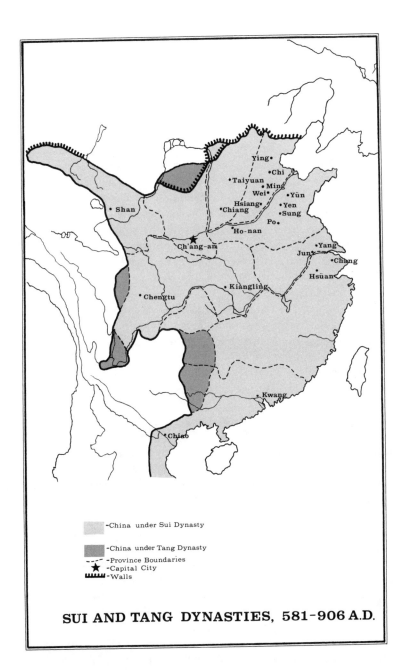

-China under Sui Dynasty

-China under Tang Dynasty

--- -Province Boundaries

★ -Capital City

ᴜᴜᴜᴜ -Walls

# SUI AND TANG DYNASTIES, 581-906 A.D.

Nestorian Christian missionaries, as well as adherents of Zoroastrianism and Islam, made their way to China and added new dimensions to Chinese culture.

More significantly, Sinicized forms of Buddhism flourished, converting many among the aristocratic Chinese. New sects appeared, notably the *T'ien-t'ai* and the *Ch'an* schools. The latter preached meditation as the path to knowledge and became the forerunner of Zen, a significant form of Buddhism in Japan. Buddhist monasteries acquired title to vast tracts of land in the Chinese countryside over which they enjoyed an extraordinary autonomy. In time monastic wealth became a problem for the imperial administration and a target for persecution by some rulers. Nevertheless, Buddhism reached its zenith in China during the T'ang period, and from China the religion passed to the Koreans and Japanese.

The government sought to deal with the age-old problem of land hunger by reviving the ancient well-field system and distributing public lands among the vastly-increased number of tax-paying peasants as soon as each reached adult status. Government subsidies further assisted China's farmers. The T'ang made no effort, however, to break up the estates of large landowners. Despite providing some relief for small cultivators, the well-field system in the long run could not cope with the continued rise in population and collapsed after the fall of the T'ang.

Several significant innovations were made in the spheres of administration and governmental operations. First, although the T'ang drew upon patterns and institutions established under the Han, they did improve organization by the creation of new offices to handle imperial affairs. Secondly, the regime published a code of laws which served as a model not only for later Chinese codes but also for those drawn up in Japan and Annam. Finally, it encouraged a major change in the method of recruitment for state service. While the bureaucracy continued to be staffed largely on the basis of family and other connections, the trend during T'ang times was clearly for men increasingly to enter the government through an elaborate system of state-run examinations. Candidates competed in four sessions, the last of which they took in the imperial palace itself. The *chin-shih* degree ("advanced scholar worthy of government appointment") represented the highest possible attainment. By the end of the dynasty, not only were the majority of high officials in the land products of this system, but enormous honor and prestige had come to be attached to successfully passing the various tests.

The military, political, and economic successes of the T'ang era inspired a flowering of Chinese culture characterized by the haunting poetry of Li Po and Tu Fu and Buddhist themes in both painting and sculpture. The perfection of block printing produced the first books probably by the seventh century (although the oldest printed text we have from China dates from 868), almost seven centuries before a similar development in Western Europe. Perhaps the rebuilding of Ch'ang-an, the imperial capital, represented the most dramatic symbol of T'ang accomplishment. A city of two million inhabitants and almost as large as modern-day Paris, Ch'ang-an was laid out as a rectangle, with streets running at right angles in a gridiron pattern. Foreign visitors marveled at its cosmopolitan character and splendor; the Japanese, in fact, copied its basic lines for their first permanent capitals at Nara and Kyoto.

The T'ang dynasty weakened in the final century and a half of its existence when population growth, having overtaxed the well-field system, created unbearable rural problems and inordinate wealth corrupted the court, the scholars, and the imperial army. Also, frontier defenses decayed and allowed barbarians to invade China once again. The T'ang finally succumbed in the opening years of the tenth century.

## • The Rise of the Sung (960-1270)

With the collapse of the T'ang dynasty, China found herself once again without effective central government. In the north, which soon would fall behind the south in population, cultural attainment, productivity, and wealth, several states known as the Five Dynasties stole the political spotlight from one another in rapid succession over the next fifty years. In the south the situation was worse in one respect yet better in another: there were twice as many states (the so-called Ten Kingdoms), yet their longer histories provided a greater degree of stability to politics and society at large.

Ironically, however, it was a northern regime, the Sung, which restored centralized government to the whole of China in the third quarter of the tenth century. Taking advantage of the achievements of one of the preceding short-lived dynasties in the region (Later Chou), the Sung gradually incorporated the formerly independent states of northern and southern China into their empire. With the aid of a bureaucracy more intricate than that of any previous dynasty, whose members now were drawn predominantly from examination candidates chosen after intense competition, the Sung could provide more uniform, capable, and effective leadership both on the local and national levels. While some criticism was leveled at the examination system for encouraging impracticality and pedantry in successful candidates, the admittedly scanty statistical evidence shows that the system did provide a channel for upward social mobility without producing a self-perpetuating elite. Perhaps thirty percent of all who passed became the first of their families to do so.

In spite of the prosperity which an expanding economy soon brought to Sung China, social problems remained the most pressing domestic concern of the rulers. A monotonously recurrent feature of Chinese life, however, worsened the plight of the peasant. The small farmer could not compete with a growing number of large landowners whose capital resources allowed them not only to acquire more and more land but, through investment in reclamation and irrigation projects and new implements, to derive greater productivity from their estates.

As pressure on the domestic scene increased, so too did threats from belligerent neighboring states. In the northeast, the Khitan tribes of Manchuria united to form the state of Liao in 907. Taking advantage of the political disunity of northern China during the period of the Five Dynasties, the Liao carved out a kingdom for themselves that included some territory on the Chinese side of the Great Wall. Conflict between the Liao and the Sung continued intermittently until 1004, when both sides negotiated a treaty that called for the frequent exchange of envoys, development of trade, and respect for the current borders between their respective territories. In addition, the Sung agreed to pay an annual tribute to the Liao — a reversal of traditional Chinese practice. This method of appeasement was used again in 1044 to deal with the Tanguts of the northwest.

The burden of these substantial tribute payments, along with the enormous expense of the military forces necessary to protect the northern frontiers, proved so onerous that the government sought to extract more taxation. The population, however, failed to respond in the way the regime wanted. The peasants could not help, because they had nothing to give; the merchants and landowners would not cooperate, because they jealously guarded their wealth. As a result, revenues fell, black marketeering grew, and society verged on rebellion.

At this point, in 1069, the emperor appointed an official by the name of Wang An-shih to become prime minister and carry out needed reforms. Wang enacted measures that effectively procured supplies for the court (a money-saving effort), offered loans to small farmers at interest rates lower than those of the moneylenders, and established a neighborhood militia system (the *pao-chia*) that improved rural security. He also reformed the bureaucracy, which, as a good Confucian, he knew to be essential to effective authority. In this area he stressed the Imperial University as the best place for training bureaucrats and revised the examinations so that they would test the candidate's practical knowledge of government and problems of administration. On the lower levels, Wang instituted salaries and corporal punishments for non-degree holding personnel in order to keep them on the virtuous path. The outcry against Wang led to his resignation after seven years in office. His reforms remained in effect until the death of the emperor who had supported him, but the new government repealed his entire program. Whether Wang's ideas would have worked is difficult to determine, but because they were never effectively implemented China made little progress toward solving her fundamental problems. The outbreak of peasant rebellion in several provinces and the failure to beat back the Jürchids (a new power in the northeast) who invaded in 1125, are ample proof of this. As a result, Sung control collapsed in the northern half of China. Withdrawing to the Huai and Yangtze valleys, the Sung set up their new capital in Hangchow and maintained the dynasty until 1279. The rest of China, however, would remain subject to alien domination for more than two centuries.

Faced with an ever-present threat from barbarian tribes to the north, the Southern Sung (as the dynasty was now called) became increasingly self-centered and less receptive to alien elements in their society and culture. One example of this changed mood was the rejection of Buddhism as a foreign religion by intellectuals who turned once again to their native Confucianism for inspiration. But Sung thinkers soon discovered that Confucianism had changed substantially over the previous centuries. As a result, they undertook to re-examine the basic texts and reinterpret their contents. The product of their effort was a synthesis known as Neo-Confucianism, with Chu Hsi as its most notable exponent. By incorporating both Taoist and even some Buddhist elements into his philosophy, he broadened and enriched Confucian concepts to explain man's relationship to the universe. While creating a new orthodoxy, however, Chu Hsi continued to emphasize virtuous behavior and subservience to superiors, two ideas which provided ideological justification for the increasing authoritarianism of Sung politics.

While many people have criticized the Sung dynasty for its failure to preserve the empire's territorial integrity, it is important to note that in many respects Chinese civilization reached its apogee during the Sung centuries. Art, literature, and technology (including the priceless invention of printing) all reached a peak of development. This was an age when artisans produced some of China's finest porcelain; when writers like Su Tung-po praised wine, women, and song in exquisite poetic style; when painters drew some of the most beautiful landscapes; and when Ssu-ma

Kuang wrote his monumental *History as a Mirror* to chronicle thirteen centuries of China's past.

Under the Sung, China also almost achieved significant sea power. Thanks to a marked increase in the productivity of the country's economy and to improvements in maritime technology (especially the invention of the compass), the volume of foreign trade rose beyond anything experienced before. For the first time sea ports rather than inland cities, which connected the overland trade routes, became the centers for China's contact with the outside world. In many respects, the Chinese seemed on the verge of an experience similar to the Commercial Revolution in Western Europe in a slightly later period. But the potential for the empire to become a world power, to carry its culture across the seas and in turn be influenced by distant cultures, was never realized.

## • China Under the Mongols (1279-1368)

During the period of Southern Sung rule, which proved to be an exceptionally peaceful and prosperous time, the northern half of China continued to live under barbarian occupation. As we have seen, first the Khitans of the Liao dynasty and then the Jürchids of the Chin dynasty succeeded in controlling all or part of that region. Finally, the Mongols swept out of the steppe to engulf northern China and spread untold death, suffering, and destruction. Since the barbarian occupations weighed most heavily on that region and because the plains area had suffered terribly from the flooding of the Yellow River at the end of the twelfth century, North China lay in ruins for nearly a century.

The Chinese in the south might have continued to live undisturbed had their rulers not become involved in the problems of the north. Around 1215, the Jürchids appealed for Sung assistance against the Mongols who had already driven them out of Peking. The Sung emperor dispatched infantry in response. Later, after the Mongols had overwhelmed the Jürchids in 1234, the Sung foolishly attempted to reconquer North China. Kublai Khan, who would succeed to the Mongol throne in 1256, promptly launched an invasion of the south. The fighting dragged on for decades before the relentless steppe warriors finally subdued the region in 1279. For the first time the whole of China was ruled by nomads who had not been previously Sinicized and who, despite adopting Chinese institutions and techniques and using Chinese to help administer the country, always remained totally alien.

As the new rulers of China, the Mongols faced the task of administering not only a vast and heavily-populated country but also one with cultural and institutional features at total variance with their own. Accustomed to ruling from the saddle over a relatively primitive and tribally-organized society, what were the Mongols to do with China? At first there was some support for destroying Chinese society, annihilating most of the population, and turning the land into a gigantic pasturage more suited to the nomadic Mongol lifestyle. But the conquerors soon perceived the advisability of leaving the Chinese and their system basically intact to exploit the country more effectively. Thus, the Mongols established an administrative apparatus essentially similar to that which the Chinese had developed. While filling lower-level posts largely with Chinese, the Mongols nevertheless kept all high offices and other important positions for themselves. Furthermore, they tended to make greater use of non-degree holding personnel and foreigners (recall the career of Marco Polo, the Venetian traveler) rather than members of the Chinese elite whom they trusted very little.

The ruling Mongol minority sought to avoid assimilation by clearly relegating the Chinese to secondary social positions. Yet, Kublai Khan himself, greatly influenced by Chinese advisers, ruled as much like a Chinese emperor as a traditional Mongol chieftain. He dutifully performed the Confucian imperial rites, took a Chinese name for his dynasty (Yüan), and even reinstituted the examination system, although examinations were held only once until late in the dynasty.

Because of its exploitive, alien character and relatively short duration, Mongol rule in China did not leave any lasting imprint on the country; yet, the conquest was not entirely without positive results. For one thing, the choice of Peking as the new capital of China made that city one of the country's most important administrative, economic, and military centers, which it has remained to this day. Secondly, the Pax Mongolica, which stretched very nearly from the Mediterranean to the Pacific Ocean at its peak, enormously stimulated and facilitated overland travel and trade between China and the West. Furthermore, the West received a great flow of Chinese technical and scientific inventions, including printing and gunpowder, which would enormously affect European society.

The first two emperors of the Yüan dynasty, Kublai Khan and his grandson Timur, proved capable and effective rulers, but their successors were incompetent and too much given to a debauched life at court. Misrule, fratricidal conflict that saw seven emperors on the throne during the last twenty-two years of the dynasty, mismanagement of the country's finances, a series of military defeats, and widespread famine in North China caused by the frequent flooding of the Yellow River contributed to the outbreak of popular revolts in the 1360s all across the country. In 1368, unable any longer to hold on to their conquest, the Mongols withdrew swiftly to the steppe. With their ouster, the Ming, a new *Chinese* dynasty, succeeded in uniting the whole of China under native rule for the first time in four hundred years.

### • The Restoration of Chinese Rule Over China: The Ming (1368-1644)

Chu Yüan-chang, the leader of the successful revolt against the Mongols, stemmed from humble origins. In fact, he was the first peasant to establish a dynasty (the Ming) in a millenium and a half. His education was informal, which perhaps contributed to his lifelong scorn for intellectuals, yet he had enormous organizational skills and proved astute enough to see the value of recruiting some learned men to assist in administering the territories that he conquered and the state that he would ultimately rule. A man who knew how to handle other men, his harsh and autocratic character had an indelible effect on the dynasty which he founded.

Despotism, in fact, became one of the hallmarks of Ming rule. It resulted in part from new institutional arrangements inaugurated at the very beginning of the dynasty by which emperors exercised enormous and direct responsibility for everyday decisions. It also resulted from the tradition of terrorism, surveillance, and frequent purges which the first emperor established.

As a consequence of the increased authority of the emperors and, later on, their closest advisers and eunuchs, the bureaucracy suffered an erosion of its influence at the upper levels. The early establishment of Neo-Confucianism as the officially-sanctioned ideology further encouraged this tendency. Ordering the publication of a new edition of the Confucian *Classics* with the commentaries of Chu Hsi, the government declared these writings to be the corpus of orthodox thought. When one recalls that the *Classics* formed the basis of the examination system which provided the bureaucracy with its membership, the full impact of this action becomes clear. Furthermore, the government revised the examinations themselves in a way that encouraged conformity through what was called the "Eight-Legged Essay." Originally designed to assist candidates to organize their thoughts, before long the essay's format severely stifled originality on the examinations and placed a premium on rote memorization and stylistics.

All in all, these measures not only harnessed the bureaucracy but also, considering the increased insecurity of official life, helped transform it into a closed, privileged institution whose members were more interested in self-preservation than in the betterment of society.

Chu Yüan-chang and his successors, consciously trying to recapture the glories of T'ang times, created a stable, prosperous, and militarily strong China that once again dominated East Asia. Less threatened from the outside than at any time since the early T'ang period, the Ming sent tribute-seeking fleets of gigantic size as far as Java, the coasts of India, the Persian Gulf, and even the east coast of Africa in the early 1400s. At the same time, some of the empire's neighbors, like Korea, became loyal tributary states, or like Japan, sought trading opportunities with this majestic power.

The early Ming period represented a time of feverish activity and forward movement. The new dynasty reopened and enlarged the long-neglected Grand Canal connecting Peking with the Yangtze valley, rebuilt a portion of the Great Wall, and planned and constructed the city of Peking in its modern form. That city became the capital of China in 1421, when the Yung-lo Emperor ordered three great walls constructed to protect it. A huge outer fortification enclosed the imperial palace wall, which in turn surrounded the red wall of the "Forbidden City." The emperor's palace lay within, its two thousand rooms and spacious grounds staffed by ten thousand servants. All structures faced southward, away from threatened frontiers. Skillful use of space separating the various buildings created the illusion of ascension to Heaven itself as one approached the abode of the ruler of the "Celestial Empire."

Culturally the Ming period witnessed a substantial effort to produce variations largely on traditional themes and forms, but at the same time one can detect the birth of what John T. Meskill, the American historian, calls a "modern temper." Whether it was the interest of Wang Yang-ming in the workings of the human mind, the proliferation of academies in the sixteenth century, the challenge to tradition and convention by the likes of the eccentric Li Chih, the introduction of spontaneity, action, and sensuality in literature (particularly in novels and dramas), or the favorable treatment accorded Christian missionaries who began to arrive shortly after the Portuguese first appeared off the south China coast, one can see in the Ming Chinese a vitality, dissatisfaction, anti-conventionalism, and even individualism that might have led to many of the same kinds of changes in China that had occurred in Western Europe during the late Middle Ages and the Renaissance. Why this "modern temper" failed to take root and blossom is a question with an enormously complex answer,

The Gate of Heavenly Peace dominates T'ien-an-men Square in Peking, often the site for ceremonial marches and gatherings.

but one that is probably tied intimately to the fate of the Ming dynasty itself. Suffice it to suggest that in the sixteenth century the Chinese seemed to have a chance to throw off at least some of the constraints of tradition and strike out in new directions. Their failure to sustain what seemed so promising may go a long way toward explaining their traumatic experience with the West in the nineteenth century.

For two centuries Ming China thrived. Then by the early part of the 1600s a number of developments began to disrupt the normal workings of government and society. First, there was a growing failure of leadership. Factionalism and intense bureaucratic partisanship, the enormous expansion of eunuch power, and the indifference of many of the emperors made misgovernment an inevitability. Second, China lost both Annam and

Burma as a result of uprisings in these tributary states, while two Japanese invasions of Korea, although repulsed by Chinese troops, placed a heavy burden on the imperial treasury. So too did attacks from the north by Mongols and raids all along the China coast by Japanese pirates and Chinese outlaws. Third, the perennial problem of creeping landlordism, particularly in the Yangtze area and the south, led to a considerable number of peasant revolts. Fourth, a doubling of the population caused pressure on the empire's land resources that could not be eased by the repopulation of the formerly devastated northern regions. Finally, increasing governmental incompetence, corruption, arbitrariness, and insensitivity served to alienate most Chinese intellectuals. The growing power of the eunuchs, whose number reached about 100,000, was especially abhorrent to the bureaucratic class.

## ● Imperial China at Her Peak: The Manchus (1644-ca. 1800)

For several generations during the late sixteenth and early seventeenth centuries, a tribe of barbarians known as the Manchus was quietly becoming a unified military power in the southern part of Manchuria. Through diplomacy and conquest a young Manchu chieftain named Nurhachi slowly brought the clans together under his leadership. By the time he was ready to challenge Ming rule over China, Nurhachi's Manchus were already imbued with Chinese culture, had developed Chinese-inspired administrative practices and institutions, and enjoyed the support of large numbers of Chinese farmers who had settled beyond the Great Wall and Chinese officials who had defected from the Ming.

Ever since 1616, when Nurhachi adopted the title of emperor and founded his own dynasty (at that time called the Latter Chin, the same name taken by the Jürchids who had earlier driven the Sung out of North China), the Manchus had been planning to attack the Ming. Nurhachi died before fulfilling his dream, but his successors continued to work toward the day when a Manchu would sit on the "Dragon Throne." In the 1640s, with the Ming beset by massive internal rebellion, the opportunity came for which the Manchus had waited patiently. In the face of little opposition, they took Peking in 1644 and then swept through the rest of the country. Ming loyalists continued to hold out in remoter areas of the south (especially Taiwan), but eventually they too were destroyed.

Paradoxically, imperial China reached the zenith and the nadir of her development while ruled by the Manchus, who adopted the dynastic title of Ch'ing. Under three emperors (K'ang-hsi, Yung-cheng, and Ch'ien-lung), who must rank with the greatest ever to hold that position during China's extensive history, the empire enjoyed extraordinarily long (1661-1796) and dynamic leadership. The results were impressive. On the domestic scene, peace and stability provided the background for such prosperity that under the Ch'ien-lung Emperor taxes were canceled on several occasions. Trade continued to expand throughout the period and handicraft industries proved enormously productive in both quantity and range of commodities. Internationally, the Manchus were especially successful. Brilliant military campaigns extended the empire to Mongolia, much of Central Asia, and Tibet. In the south, Burma, Annam, and Nepal fell under Chinese domination as well.

To ensure the success of their dynasty, the Manchus sought to become "more Chinese than the Chinese." They made few changes in the Ming administrative system (except to balance Chinese officials with Manchus as a controlling mechanism) and, perhaps more importantly, passed themselves off as protectors of Chinese civilization. The examination system, with its Neo-Confucian basis, remained an integral part of the political and social setting. The emperors, particularly K'ang-hsi and Ch'ien-lung, patronized scholarly endeavors, which included some of the most monumental projects ever undertaken anywhere (such as the *Complete Library in Four Branches of Literature* in 36,000 manuscript volumes). They also attempted to become ideal Confucian rulers by assiduously practicing the proper rites and writing and painting in the manner of the scholar-bureaucratic elite. Nevertheless, the Manchus remained very concious of their non-Chinese origins and strove to retain their identity by forbidding intermarriage with Chinese, banning Chinese settlement in Manchuria, and prohibiting the adoption of certain Chinese customs (such as foot-binding), while preserving the Manchu language.

By the end of the eighteenth century, in spite of outward signs of continuing stability and prosperity, much was beginning to change for the worse in China. Many of the problems that surfaced in the new century were the same that had plagued dynasties through China's long history. But to those perennial problems would be added a new factor — the intrusion of the West — which eventually proved so disruptive that it would contribute more than anything else to the end not merely of the Ch'ing dynasty but of the entire imperial system itself and practically all of the traditions and values that gave it meaning.

# 2

# China's Collision with the West (1800-1912)

AT THE BEGINNING of the nineteenth century, many non-Chinese regarded China as the mightiest empire in the world. Asian neighbors eagerly sent tribute, while countless Western intellectuals lauded her for being a society run by those best able to govern and guided by a natural morality. Such adulation, however, was the result of misunderstanding, willful self-deception, or a distorted sense of Chinese reality. In truth, fearful of assimilation and increasingly on the defensive, the Manchus were fast losing their hold on Chinese society. Population pressure and land hunger, China's perennial problems, were once again threatening to disrupt domestic harmony. Already the portents were ominous, and rebellion was in the wind. Furthermore, the bureaucratic elite had become a haven for the privileged and ambitious. Too much corruption and too little dedication among its members undercut the efficiency and effectiveness of local administration and would contribute enormously to the outbreak of rural discontent. When the Europeans finally kicked in the doors of old China, they would be amazed to find so much decay, and the empire, hitherto greatly admired, would reveal itself to be weak and moribund.

In the Western European nations China found herself face to face with a civilization whose values, attitudes, institutions, and general world view were totally different from her own. What is more, she was confronted by people who refused to play her game, who not only wanted to ignore the old rules but arrogantly sought to draw up the new ones unilaterally. Thinking these barbarians to be similar to all the others who had crossed her threshold over the centuries, China expected them to recognize her as the Middle Kingdom, while acknowledging the emperor as the Son of Heaven and paying him homage, and to absorb Chinese ways. But these barbarian "ocean devils" came by way of the sea — going and coming as they wished, making assimilation difficult — instead of overland as heretofore. The total inability of China to make the Europeans heed her traditions and the humiliation which resulted from her attempts to do so, proved so traumatic that traditional Chinese self-confidence was irrevocably shattered. The collapse of the Manchu dynasty, the end of the imperial system, and the emergence of Chinese nationalism all developed as direct results of this tragic experience.

## ● The Violent Opening of China

By an imperial decree issued in 1757, the Western presence in China at the beginning of the nineteenth century was limited to merchants permitted to ply their trade solely in the port of Canton. Required to live within special compounds, or factories, the British, French, Dutch, and later American traders conducted their business through a committee of thirteen Chinese merchants known as the *Cohong.* Residing in Canton was not easy for the Westerners. They labored under all sorts of restrictions that affected not only their business dealings but also their private affairs. Thus, they were prohibited from employing Chinese servants, rowing on the Pearl River which flowed past the city, and bringing their wives to China. All in all, the Chinese treated them as was to be expected; moreover, the Westerners were merchants and foreigners trying to peddle goods for which the Chinese really had no need. Their confinement to Canton, then, amounted to dispensing charity to beggars at the back door.

In 1834 an event occurring in far-off Britain set in motion an effort to change the Canton system. The House of Commons in that year voted to cancel the commercial monopoly hitherto held by the East India Company in China. With passage of the bill, any English businessman with goods and capital could now participate in the China trade. Yet, without substantial change in the way the Chinese were willing to do business with the West, there was little chance that private traders would be able to take advantage of what had been granted to them by their own government. With this in mind, a newly-appointed British superintendent of trade, Sir Charles Napier, tried to negotiate a commercial treaty with the Chinese viceroy of Canton. His effort was in vain largely because the viceroy saw no reason for altering an arrangement which was rooted in the traditional

Chinese tributary system and which profited many of his subordinates personally.

Soon, however, another factor contributed to increasing tensions between the Westerners and the Chinese: the opium trade. As an import, opium had been arriving in coastal ports of the empire from India long before any Westerners had become involved in the China trade. The dubious honor of being the first European shippers of the drug belonged to the Portuguese, but during the last quarter of the eighteenth century, despite repeated imperial decrees prohibiting the importation of opium, British agents had taken over the trade. By 1800 the volume of opium being sold in China was substantial; in the 1830s it increased markedly at over five million pounds annually. Consequently, Napier tried to convince the Chinese to legalize the drug traffic, but the government refused his request, denouncing the use of opium as a menace to public health and a drain on China's reserves of precious metals. On both counts the throne's concern proved well-founded. In the first instance, the drug was having a particularly deleterious effect on China's elite; in the second, from 1831 to 1836 opium imports had produced an estimated loss of thirty million taels of silver to the royal treasury.

The issue finally reached the crisis stage at the end of the decade. In 1839, after having called for and received opinions from various officials, the emperor appointed a ranking bureaucrat, Lin Tse-hsü, as commissioner at Canton and ordered him to put an end to the trade in "foreign mud," as the Chinese sarcastically called opium. Taking a hard line against continuation of the drug traffic, Lin forced the foreigners to surrender the approximately twenty thousand chests stored in the Canton factories; thereupon, with great public display, he had it all destroyed. The British superintendent of trade, Sir Charles Elliot, condemned this action as unjustified confiscation of property and helped to convince the authorities in England that what Lin had done constituted an attack against the British crown. Hostilities between the two countries commenced almost immediately.

For the first time barbarians assaulted China from the sea. The British fleet, supplied from Singapore, bombarded Canton and then proceeded northward along the coast, easily destroying or dispersing the Chinese war junks sent against it. Unable to match Western arms and apparently unwilling to mobilize the forces at their disposal, the Manchus sued for peace in 1842. The Treaty of Nanking, signed in that year, called for the opening of five ports — Canton, Amoy, Foochow, Ningpo, and Shanghai — to trade, and implicitly recognized the legal equality of foreign states with China by permitting consuls to reside in those same cities. The

Chinese also ceded the island of Hong Kong, agreed to regulate tariffs (set later at five percent), and gave in to the demand for an indemnity equal to twenty-one million pounds sterling. New agreements forced upon the Chinese in 1843-1844 by the British and Americans added two more features to the new relationship between China and the West soon known as the treaty system: a "most-favored nation" clause, which stipulated that further concessions made to any one country would be shared by all, and "extraterritoriality," which granted to Westerners the right to be governed by their own nations' laws while residing in China.

For the long-term development of Sino-Western relations, these early treaties were ominous signs of future trouble for China. Tragically, the Chinese generally failed to comprehend the full implication of these documents. Rather than learn from the bitter experience of defeat, they preferred to pretend not only that little had changed but that in fact what had changed should be viewed as a Chinese victory of sorts. This thinking is clearly illustrated by the interpretation which the Chinese applied to the two most important concessions granted to the Westerners: most-favored nation treatment and extraterritoriality. Very simply stated, they viewed both as reformulations of traditional Chinese practices for handling barbarians. The former, it was argued, would permit the government to play off foreigner against foreigner ("barbarians against barbarians") to China's ultimate benefit; the latter would appease the barbarians and perhaps dissuade them from making any further demands. Even taking all of the concessions into consideration, the Chinese convinced themselves that they had managed to confine the foreigners to China's periphery and thereby keep them from interfering in the country's internal affairs.

Yet, if the Chinese understood the treaties of the early 1840s to be the end to concessions, the Westerners saw them as merely the first steps toward the goal of opening the interior of China to Western diplomatic, business, and cultural interests. Such conflicting views ensured the probability of future military clashes.

After slightly more than a decade of peace, the inevitable occurred with the outbreak in 1856 of the Second Opium War, or Arrow War as it is often called. At the end of four years of sporadic fighting the Europeans triumphed again and vengefully burned the Summer Palace of the emperor. The signing of the Treaty of Peking in 1860 opened the interior of China to Western merchants and missionaries, required the Chinese to accept permanent diplomatic representation in Peking, and granted certain additional territorial concessions to both the British and the Russians.

U. S. S. R.

Lake Baikal

Lake Balkhash

PEOPLES REPUBLIC OF MONGOLIA

Urumchi

Sinkiang Uighur Autonomous Region

Kansu

Inner Mongolia Autonomous Region

Heilungkiang

Harbin

Changchun

Kirin

Mukden

Liaoning

Peking

Hopei

Tientsin

Paotow

Yellow

Taiyuan

Yenan

Shansi

Tsinan

Shantung

KOREA

Ningsia Hui Aut. Region

Sining

Lanchow

Yellow

Loyang

Kaifeng

Chengchow

Kiangsu

Chinghai

Sian

Honan

Anhwei

Nanking

Shanghai

Tibet Autonomous Region

Shensi

Hupeh

Hofei

Hangchow

Lhasa

Chamdo

Chamdo Area

Chengtu

Szechwan

Wuhan

Chungking

Yangtze R.

Chekiang

Nanchang

NEPAL

SIKKIM

BHUTAN

Changsha

Kiangsi

Hunan

Foochow

Fukien

E. PAKISTAN

Kweiyang

Kweichow

Kwangsi Chuang Aut. Region

Kwangtung

FORMOSA (TAIWAN)

INDIA

Kunming

Yunnan

Nanning

Canton

Hong Kong (Br.)

Macao (Port.)

BURMA

N. VIETNAM

Hainan Island

LAOS

- The Grand Canal
**Kansu** – Province
Sian  – Major city
**SIKKIM** – Adjacent nation
- - - – Provincial boundary
- The Great Wall

miles
0   100 200      500

# MODERN CHINA

Many Chinese blamed the Manchus for their problems with the Europeans, arguing that military defeats and humiliating concessions were all signs that the dynasty had lost its right to rule. As far as the imperial court was concerned, however, the barbarians represented less of a threat to its survival than the shattering explosions of domestic rebellion at mid-century.

## •Domestic Rebellion and the Taiping

Since Western penetration of China largely disturbed only the coastal areas of the empire, its effect on the Chinese people living in the interior remained minimal. Of greater concern to most Chinese were a number of domestic developments which, taken together, were producing intolerable living conditions in several major regions. Causes of distress included inflation, unemployment, famine, natural disasters, and corruption and inefficiency in the bureaucracy. By the middle of the nineteenth century the country was ripe for a major eruption of popular unrest. As it turned out, three sizeable rebellions would rock the empire from the 1850s to the 1870s: the Nien (1853-1868) in the region between the Huai and Yellow Rivers; the Muslim (1855-1878) in the southwest and northwest provinces; and above all, the Taiping (1850-1864), engulfing much of south and central China. The Taiping, a threat to the very survival of the dynasty, deserves close scrutiny.

Hung Hsiu-ch'üan, the son of a peasant couple living in wretched conditions outside of Canton, was the future leader of the Taiping movement. His family descended from a group known as the Hakkas, a minority people who had fled to southern China to escape the Manchus at the time of their invasion. As the brightest of his family, Hung was given the opportunity to prepare for the civil service examinations. His first three attempts, however, resulted in failures, and following the third (1837) the strain produced a high fever and coma that lasted for forty days. During that time he reportedly dreamed that he had seen God and Christ (although at the time he did not know them as such) and that the latter, addressing him as a younger brother, ordered him to rid the world of demons. Nothing came of this experience until a few years later when, after failing to pass the examination a fourth time, he read a set of nine Christian tracts which he had received from missionaries in Canton in 1836. There he found the meaning of his dream: God had called upon him to purge China of the alien Manchu dynasty and of the baneful teachings of Confucius and to establish a theocracy called the Heavenly

Kingdom of Great Peace in their stead. Hung's ideology, as it developed over several years, presented an odd mixture of native Chinese and grotesquely distorted Christian concepts. While much of what he proclaimed sought to conserve some aspects of traditional Confucian thought, his program of land reform, abolition of private property, and equality of the sexes, if fully implemented, would have revolutionized Chinese society, because Hung sought the overthrow of the entire Confucian order.

The enormous popular support accorded to Hung and his movement, in addition to the amazing ineptitude of the imperial armies sent out against him, helps to explain the early successes of the Taiping Rebellion. But internal squabbles among the rebel leaders, strategic blunders during later military campaigns, ideological fanaticism that alienated many possible supporters (especially the elite of China), discrepancies between the theory and practice of Taiping life, and the failure to take advantage of early Western sympathy, all contributed to the movement's ultimate collapse. So too did the extraordinary efforts of a number of Chinese officials like Tseng Kuo-fan and Li Hung-chang to revitalize the defenses of the dynasty and rally new, better-equipped and organized provincial armies to its cause.

Despite its failure, the Taiping Rebellion became an inspiration to later generations of Chinese rebels and revolutionaries. In addition, it led to several major developments in imperial politics: an increase in the appointment of Chinese as opposed to Manchu officials to decision-making positions; a greater independence of action and input into imperial affairs on the part of provincial officials; and the first tentative efforts to reform and modernize Chinese society. All three would have important bearing on the fate of the Ch'ing dynasty and the imperial system itself.

## • The Restoration of the Dynasty and "Self-Strengthening" (1861-1895)

The ascension to the throne of a new emperor in 1861 inaugurated an era of high spirits and energetic activity at the imperial court. As the Taiping Rebellion subsided and the threat to the dynasty diminished, both Manchu and Chinese leaders turned their attention to the task of rehabilitating the nation. Confucian idealism, with its emphasis on good government through properly-trained and virtuous men, enjoyed a resurgence as the regime sought to attract the best it could find to fill the top posts in the bureaucracy. This idealism made the reign of the T'ung-chih Emperor (1861-1874) a period of restoration and revival.

Feng Kuei-fen, a scholar-official well-read in many areas other than the Confucian Classics, best personified the spirit of this period. In a series of essays written in 1860, Feng noted that the West was not only superior in technological and scientific capability but also ahead of China in its utilization of human and material resources. Furthermore, governments in that part of the world skillfully utilized more effective communication between themselves and their subjects. Feng regarded China's defeat at the hands of the West as the "greatest outrage since creation, which should infuriate every red-blooded person." He argued, however, against both the blind impulse to expel the Westerners and the stratagem of "using the barbarians against the barbarians." Instead, he urged that the Chinese recognize with shame their country's inferiority. "When we are ashamed," Feng wrote, "the best thing to do is strengthen ourselves." "Self-strengthening" — a phrase which he coined and which came to describe the reform era which spanned the rest of the century — could be achieved, however, only by improving upon existing Chinese institutions, making greater use of China's own human talents and economic resources, increasing the links between monarch and people, and making practice conform to ideals. These improvements would serve, of course, to restore the vitality of the Confucian system. Nevertheless, Feng made it clear that China needed to learn from the West on matters concerning technology and science. In this respect his argument anticipated Chang Chih-tung's enunciation in the 1890s of the so-called "*t'i* and *yung* dichotomy" in his famous slogan, "Chinese learning for substance [*t'i*], Western learning for function [*yung*]." This dichotomy suggests using Western means for Chinese ends, retaining Confucian values while utilizing Western tools, supporting Chinese traditional civilization while importing Western technology.

The "T'ung-chih Restoration" was, as the American historian, Mary C. Wright, argued in her study of this period, the "last stand of Chinese conservatism." The story of the restoration attempt represented the search for Confucian stability on the one hand and for modernization on the other. It concerned the efforts of an often brilliant group of conservative officials both at the imperial court (Prince Kung) and in the provinces (Tseng Kuo-fan, Li Hung-chang, and Tso Tsung-t'ang) to bring about some radical innovation *within* the old order, when in the long run what China required was a radical change of the old order itself. Faced with defects in the traditional Chinese system that should have been obvious, these conservatives set to work shoring up the nation's Confucian foundation by initiating a series of broad reforms. Aimed at a true restoration of all that was inherently useful and beneficial in the Confucian system, the reform projects unfortunately failed because they were based upon misconceptions. Adhering to the Chinese conservative tradition, the restoration leaders directed their attention largely toward administrative improvement. Preoccupation with the symptomatic abuses of the system rather than with its substantial defects produced the inevitable result.

If the restoration attempt came to an end in the early 1870s, the ideas which justified it continued to influence Chinese reformism for another decade and a half. The self-strengthening movement managed to introduce a number of reforms, but its total achievement was negligible and its ultimate objective unattained. The failure cannot be blamed exclusively on the few leaders of the movement, although they deserve some criticism for their shortsightedness. More significant in the long run was the incredible inertia of the bureaucracy as a whole. Too many officials simply refused to accept even that which the self-strengtheners realized: that the Chinese system did not function as it should. The overwhelming number of officials distrusted and opposed every innovation. Even the reformers themselves accepted change only if it was clearly advantageous and did not undermine any bulwark essential to the preservation of the old order. In the end, the self-strengtheners could not resolve the contradiction in their goals. On the one hand, they desired to transform China into a modern state able to compete effectively with the Western powers; on the other, they sought to maintain the Confucian system virtually unchanged. Unfortunately for China, the requirements of the one ran counter to those of the other.

## • Foreign Expansionism in China

When the self-strengthening movement got underway in the 1860s, it was aided by the decision of the Western powers to pursue a policy of cooperation with the Chinese government and allow it a chance to recover from the chaos and destruction which domestic rebellion had caused. Apparently satisfied with the concessions which they had already wrung from China, the Westerners sought now to ensure that nothing would endanger their treaty rights. This thinking led not only to a cessation of hostilities toward the empire but also to a conscious effort to help the Chinese revive and modernize their system.

Within less than a decade, however, a rash of anti-Christian acts in the countryside in 1869-1870 and the almost immediate renewal of Western demands on China had succeeded in undermining the cooperative policy in short order. The massacre of missionaries at Tientsin (1870), the revival of a long-standing Western request for audiences with the emperor (1873), and the murder by guerrillas of a British vice-consul near the Chinese-Burmese border (1875) launched a new period of intensified foreign imperialism. The Russian occupation of Ili in Sinkiang (1871-1881), the Japanese attack on Formosa (1874) and seizure of the Liu-ch'iu Islands (1879), the British attempt to open Yunnan province (1875), and the French seizure of Annam and the war of 1884-1885, all served to further weaken China and set the stage for the Sino-Japanese War of 1894-1895.

That conflict began as a result of a long-standing dispute between China and Japan over control of Korea, for centuries a Chinese dependency. In 1894, when a nationalist revolt known as the Tonghak Rebellion broke out in the peninsula, both the Chinese and the Japanese landed troops to restore order, fearing Russian action. In August, a Japanese fleet attacked a Chinese troopship without a declaration of war. From that moment on Japanese naval and land forces achieved one easy victory after another over their Chinese counterparts. Had Japan not feared the total collapse of China and the loss of gains she had already made, she could have occupied Peking itself. Instead, negotiations commenced leading to the signing of the Treaty of Shimonoseki in April, 1895.

According to the treaty, China had to surrender Formosa, the Pescadores Islands, and Port Arthur, and pay an indemnity to the Japanese. In addition, Korea would become independent. Before the terms of the agreement could be carried out, however, Russia, Germany, and France (the Triple Intervention) presented separate notes to the Japanese foreign minister, demanding that Port Arthur remain in Chinese hands. Each of the three powers had its own reasons for making an issue of this strategic facility: Russia feared Japanese encroachment in northern China, regarded as her own preserve; Germany sought a port on the Chinese coast to develop a sphere of influence; and France wished to cement her recently-concluded Dual Alliance with Russia. Faced with this opposition, Japan had no choice but to return Port Arthur.

Japan's defeat of China revealed the latter's military impotence, despite decades of self-strengthening measures, and triggered a mad scramble by the powers for shares of the Chinese pie before the empire collapsed. In 1897, Germany seized the Shantung port of Tsingtao, which lay at the entrance to the Yellow River valley. Russia countered by taking a lease on nearby Port Arthur. For her part, France negotiated a lease for the southern port of Kwangchow, while the British moved into Weihaiwei. One year later, Britain also claimed the entire Yangtze valley as her exclusive commercial sphere. All parties seemed resigned to the inevitability of China's wholesale partition.

At this point the United States intervened in an effort to stabilize the situation. In 1899, Secretary of State John Hay (with British encouragement) proclaimed the doctrine of the "open door." In a letter circulated among all the nations concerned, Hay called for equal commercial access throughout China and an end to spheres of influence. Although not one of the major powers committed itself to supporting the idea, Hay announced that everyone had wholeheartedly accepted it. Only Japan took issue with the American conclusion. Surprisingly enough, while the open door principle probably had no effect on the imperialists, their moves to slice up the "Chinese melon" slowed noticeably after its pronouncement. Probably fear of conflict with one another inspired their separate decisions to consolidate gains already made rather than continue to seek new spoils.

## • The Reform Movement of 1898

China's humiliating defeat at the hands of Japan and her impending dismemberment by the imperialists gave final impetus to a new method of reform that had been first broached by certain intellectuals outside the emperor's court. Their writings discussed the usual range of possible measures for improving the economic condition of the nation, but more significantly they called for radical reforms, including the abolition of the civil service examination system and the introduction of representative government. In brief, these reformers demanded basic institutional changes in contrast to the cosmetic touch-ups that had characterized the thinking of the self-strengtheners.

Spurred on by the growing mood of crisis that began sweeping the country after the mid-1890s, a handful of knowledgeable men, under the leadership of an unorthodox scholar named K'ang Yu-wei, began an all-out campaign to plead the cause of radical reformism. Making effective use of all of the traditional channels (memorials and audiences) as well as more modern means of communication (newspapers and magazines), they soon attracted the attention of the emperor himself. The climax of their effort came during a one-hundred-and-three-day period in 1898 when the emperor invited K'ang and his associates to court to institute their reform program.

In spite of K'ang's argument that there was really nothing unusual in the idea of radically changing the Chinese system (with the then provocative thesis that Confucius himself had been an innovator and had intended his philosophy to promote institutional change), he had gone too far too fast. The forces of opposition within the bureaucracy and especially at court gathered around the powerful figure of the Empress Dowager Tzu-hsi. The personification of the old order and bitterly anti-foreign since she had witnessed the burning of the Summer Palace in 1860, she may have poisoned her own son, the T'ung-chih Emperor in 1874 and then arbitrarily selected her nephew as his successor. Although not completely averse to adopting Western methods in the self-strengthening tradition, she decided to oppose the radical reformers both because of their extremism and because her own influence over the throne seemed threatened. Once she had determined to call a halt to the reforms, she moved quickly with the support of the most powerful warlord general, Yüan Shi-k'ai, and his army. K'ang Yu-wei fled for his life, but six of his colleagues were caught and put to death. The emperor, who had given the reformers so much support, was virtually deposed and spent the rest of his life in confinement. Perhaps only Western interest in his survival kept Tzu-hsi from having him eliminated altogether. Thus, the "Hundred Days of Reform" were terminated abortively.

## • The Boxer Rebellion (1900)

During the 1890s, in many areas of China, secret societies arose as centers of opposition to the alien Manchus. Toward the end of the century, however, these organizations underwent a significant change: their enmity shifted from the dynasty to the foreigners who for the past fifty years had heaped humiliation and misfortune on their country. With the encouragement of local officials, who saw in the popular mood a weapon of potential value against the imperialists, many of the secret societies began to engage in anti-Western activities. One of the most significant groups, known as the I Ho Ch'üan, or "Righteous and Harmonious Fists" ("Boxers" to the Europeans) ignited the fuse for the furious anti-foreign rebellion that erupted in 1900.

In June of that year, fearing the imperialists might restore the emperor to power, the Empress Dowager ordered provincial authorities to organize the Boxers to fight an expected foreign invasion. In the countryside fanatical bands of Boxers committed all sorts of violent acts against Westerners and their property. In Peking itself, after seeking safety in the embassy compound, the foreign community came under Boxer siege. The defenders had to hold out for fifty-five days until the arrival of an international relief force. Driving the Boxers from the capital, an allied army under the command of a German general then proceeded to smash the rebellion in the provinces.

Shattered by the Boxer catastrophe, the old Empress Dowager fled to Sian in a donkey cart, but not before ordering Li Hung-chang (one of the heroes of the anti-Taiping campaigns) to negotiate with the allies as his final official act. As revenge for the Boxer "outrage," the imperialists mercilessly imposed an indemnity of almost $334 million, fixed the tariff at five percent, ordered the immediate execution of specified Chinese officials, and permanently stationed troops in the capital. In the aftermath of the episode, China lay prostrate before her enemies, the Manchus hopelessly discredited.

Some historians today view the Boxer Rebellion as China's first significant nationalist outbreak, heralding a trend, not just in China but worldwide, that would intensify as the twentieth century progressed. Writing at the turn of the century, Sir Robert Hart, the British official who had so effectively reformed the imperial customs administration, predicted that in fifty years' time "twenty million Boxers" would terminate the unequal treaties and repay China's humiliations with interest.

## • Toward the First Chinese Revolution

In the aftermath of the Boxer Rebellion, there were few thinking Chinese who questioned the need for change. Reformers and revolutionaries argued strenuously over innovations to be pursued. Returning to the capital in 1901, the aging Empress Dowager immediately solicited advice on reform from her officials. As a consequence of the deliberations that followed, the government announced the initiation of a series of institutional changes closely resembling those proposed in 1898 by K'ang Yu-wei. This time, however, these efforts (1901-1905) would produce lasting results. The more important features of the emerging program included abolition of the civil service examinations, introduction of Western-type schools based on modern educational concepts, and the sending of students abroad. A deafening clamor for constitutional government in China, especially from students attending foreign schools, followed hard upon these events. The pressure became so great that the regime had to acquiesce. In 1908 it proposed a constitution to become effective after nine years of tutelage, culminating in a system very close to democracy. In spite of last-gasp efforts by the Manchus to preserve the government's traditional power, the mood in society was so anti-Manchu that the transition to constitutionalism seemed inevitable.

Meanwhile, for some, reform no longer held the answer to China's problems. Rooted in the tradition of China's secret societies, revolutionary organizations began to form in various locales. They attracted many of those same young people who had studied abroad only to return home to find few official jobs awaiting them and incompetent reactionaries still in charge of the government. After numerous false starts and failures, the revolution began on October 10, 1911, when a student munitions storehouse at Hankow exploded. Today the Chinese still celebrate the anniversary of this "Double Tenth" (the tenth day of the tenth month). The fall of the centuries-old imperial system followed rapidly. A newly-elected parliament meeting in Nanking chose Dr. Sun Yat-sen, a generally unsuccessful but well-known revolutionary, to be the first provisional president of the Chinese Republic.

Sun was born of a poor peasant family in 1866 in a village near Canton. At the age of thirteen he went to live with his brother, a successful merchant-farmer in Hawaii. There Sun attended a local missionary school and later graduated from Oahu College in 1883. Frequent travel between China and the islands over the next few years helped develop his revolutionary attitudes. During the late 1880s and early 1890s, he studied medicine in Canton and then Hong Kong, and upon earning his degree began to practice in Macao. All the while he was planning for the day when he would help to overthrow the Manchu dynasty. In 1895 his revolutionary activity began in earnest with travels abroad to raise money among the overseas Chinese.

As a constitutionalist, Sun Yat-sen admired the French Third Republic but looked upon Japan as the most logical model for the Chinese revolution. Japan intrigued him because she had borrowed the institutions and culture of China yet had managed successfully to modernize herself and rise to great-power status. Beyond his commitment to constitutionalism, Sun based his revolutionary thought on what he called the "Three Principles of the People:" the people's nationalism, the people's democracy, and the people's livelihood. The revolution itself, he argued, would progress through three stages: military government, political tutelage, and consitutional democracy.

When the revolution actually broke out in 1911, Sun was in the United States on one of his many fund-raising trips. Upon his return to China, the provisional assembly named him president, but a formidable rival stood in his way. Yüan Shih-k'ai, the treacherous warlord who had aided the deceased Empress Dowager in her elimination of the radical reformers in 1898, now commanded China's most powerful and disciplined army and controlled Peking. Yüan had already overthrown the Manchu dynasty, but his forces now threatened the country with civil war. Everyone feared that another outbreak of violence would enable the Westerners to impose new and more burdensome treaties upon China. Seeking to eliminate that possibility, Sun resigned his presidency in exchange for Yüan's promise to govern the republic according to the new constitution and with the national assembly. Sun's selfless act, together with Western loans and promises of future support, strengthened Yüan's position. His commitment to constitutionalism, however, soon revealed itself to be completely insincere.

# 3

# *Nationalist to Communist Revolution (1912-1949)*

HER VIOLENT COLLISION with the West in the nineteenth century had proved humiliating and traumatic for China. Mired in complacency and committed to preserving the traditional system, too many Chinese and Manchus had failed to grasp the significance of mounting Western triumphs at China's expense. Convinced that the problems either would disappear in time or could be solved by the application of centuries-old practices in barbarian relations, government leaders unwittingly signed the death warrant of both the Ch'ing dynasty and the imperial system. Reluctantly they responded to calls for change, but their efforts proved disappointingly superficial. As the twentieth century opened, growing numbers of Chinese who had lost faith in the possibility of saving their country through reform were turning to a more radical solution: revolution. But what kind of revolution? The decades after 1911 would see this question debated over and over again; and to this day it is a subject of controversy among the Chinese.

## • Yüan Shih-k'ai's Regime (1912-1916)

Yüan Shih-k'ai, destined to serve as China's first president, was born in Honan Province in 1859. Hoping to rise out of his poor peasant environment, he prepared for the civil service examination but was unsuccessful. With the bureaucracy thus closed to him, he entered the military and eventually gained favor with the Empress Dowager. In 1898, contrary to his pledge to support the emperor's program, he helped Tzu-hsi to reassert her authority and bring an end to the Hundred Days of Reform. Well aware of Yüan's penchant for trickery, the Manchu regent dismissed him after the Empress Dowager's death in 1908, but during the revolution of 1911, the government solicited his services in defense of the dynasty. At first he gave his patrons cause for hope by suppressing disorder in Hankow, but then he refused to proceed further unless appointed premier. Dictating his own terms, he treacherously forced the Manchus to abdicate and deceptively "persuaded" Sun Yat-sen to step aside as provisional president of the new republic. After he obtained loans from the great powers in return for a guarantee of their treaty rights, his position seemed unassailable. The Chinese revolution had apparently come to an end with a capable "strong man" to ensure stability.

Yüan, however, nurtured greater aspirations than the presidency of a liberal republic. Remaining in Peking on the pretext of keeping order in the capital, he refused to cooperate in 1913 with the national assembly in Nanking, where Sun Yat-sen's party (the Kuomintang, KMT, National People's Party, or Nationalists) held the majority. When the assembly delegates protested, Yüan attacked Nanking and dispersed them. Sun departed for Japan where he would remain in exile until after Yüan's death in 1916. With his opposition out of the way, Yüan scrapped the constitution and proclaimed himself president for life. China now found herself ruled by a virtual military dictatorship as Yüan edged closer to his ultimate ambition – the ascension of the Dragon Throne.

Yüan had powerful enemies, however, in the increasingly aggressive Japanese. Since 1905 Japan had dominated East Asia, partitioning Manchuria and Mongolia with the Russians and annexing Korea. As an ally of the British at the outbreak of World War I in August, 1914, she easily took the German concessions in Shantung and several islands in the southwest Pacific. Many Japanese, who had supported the more malleable Sun, regarded the warlord Yüan's capture of the Chinese Revolution as a threat to Japan's interests. In January, 1915, with China at her mercy, Japan presented Yüan with the infamous "Twenty-One Demands," intending to reduce the young republic to satellite status. Among other terms, the document called for extension of Japanese leases on Chinese railways and mines, exclusive rights in the Yangtze valley, and installation of Japanese advisers in the Chinese government. Despite a flood of Chinese popular protest, Yüan accepted (with U.S. support) an altered version of the original stipulations in a treaty signed with Japan toward the end of May.

With the Japanese temporarily appeased, Yüan moved towards his intended goal — the founding of a new imperial dynasty. After months of public preparation, he announced that his reign as emperor would commence in 1916. Protest arose from all quarters. Students, businessmen, and peasants voiced their hatred of the perennially opportunistic Yüan and his betrayal of the republic. Even army officers now sought to oust him. The storm of opposition finally drove Yüan to renounce the throne and withdraw from politics. Within six months he died an embittered man. Yet, far from improving China's political situation, Yüan's ouster left a vacuum in national politics which no successor could adequately fill. In the absence of strong central government in Peking (where the fiction of republicanism was preserved), local warlords with private armies emerged in numbers too large to count. Their separatist ambitions as well as lack of commitment to republicanism and nationalism kept China politically fragmented and internationally weak for well over three decades. For his part, Sun Yat-sen would struggle in vain over the next few years to establish a workable government in Canton as a base from which to lead the struggle for national unification.

## • The Intellectual Revolution and New Culture Movement (1917-1923)

The twentieth century has witnessed the collapse of traditional China. The first blow was struck when revolutionaries not only overthrew the Ch'ing dynasty but also signaled the death of the imperial institution itself with the establishment of the republic. Even though the new political order failed to survive the machinations of Yüan Shih-k'ai and the disruptive acts of the warlords, there was little sentiment among thinking Chinese for a restoration of traditional politics. As their enthusiasm carried them further to the left, many withdrew support even from the republic, thus demolishing any possible return to monarchy.

The reason for this attitude is not hard to find. A new generation of intellectuals, Western-educated or at least Western-influenced, had emerged to challenge not merely the old politics but also the whole philosophical basis of traditional China. As yet politically impotent, the progressives nevertheless wielded enormous influence over a growing reading public, which was increasingly willing to ponder radical solutions to China's problems. Western standards became the yardstick by which the "new men" judged China, and Western political institutions, culture, scientific knowledge, and technology promised the means by which they sought to forge a modern nation.

To achieve the complete transformation of national life, men like Ch'en Tu-hsiu, Ts'ai Yüan-p'ei, and Hu Shih (products of American education) called upon their countrymen to abolish all vestiges of the past. Unlike previous reformers, they had no desire to purify or revitalize Confucianism; rather, they strove to discredit it as a reactionary, obscurant philosophy whose continued domination of Chinese society would only further impede the country's progress. To replace Confucian ideas, the new men published magazines (*New Youth, New Tide,* and *Weekly Critic*) in which they offered a tantalizing array of Western substitutes, including the philosophies of Kant, Nietzsche, Dewey, Bergson, and Marx. In the short space of a few years, Chinese were introduced to ideas and systems of thought which had taken Europeans more than a century to develop and digest. For the time being, few people made a personal commitment to any particular philosophy. Most merely dabbled in the vast reservoir of Western wisdom available for the first time. To be sure, there was much foolishness, as the glorification of science exemplifies, but finally the debates and controversies that flourished in those years had two major consequences: they enormously stimulated the thinking public in China and strengthened nationalist sentiment, and they popularized such notions as progress, democracy, freedom, and individualism, particularly through the new magazines whose editors and writers abandoned classical Chinese in favor of the vernacular (*pai-hua*).

## • The Search for National Unification (1916-1926)

Together with the intellectual revolution which was sweeping China, developments at the Paris Peace Conference (convened in 1919 to conclude the post-World War I settlements) contributed to the growing activism of many Chinese in the early 1920s. The Chinese had hoped to obtain some revision of the unequal treaties by their participation in the war on the side of the victorious allies. If nothing else, they felt certain that Germany's concessions would be returned to China and, if the slogans "territorial integrity" and "national self-determination" as proclaimed by many of the world's statesmen had any substance, perhaps one could expect even more. However, because of a secret agreement signed in early 1917 by England, France, and the warlord government in Peking to turn over Germany's Shantung holdings to Japan, Chinese hopes were frustrated. The revelation of allied duplicity released a torrent of protest among incredulous Chinese of all classes that culminated in a major eruption on

May 4, 1919. While this public outcry had little effect on China's relations with the outside world, it represented a significant step forward in the growth of Chinese nationalism. Many people received their initial taste of political activity by participating in the strikes, demonstrations, and boycotts that swept the country (particularly its urban centers) as part of what became known as the "May Fourth Movement."

Perhaps more than anything else, party politics in China benefited from the spirit of activism which now pervaded society. Hundreds flocked to Sun Yat-sen and his Kuomintang, revitalizing it after years of precarious existence, while a select few also joined the newly-formed (1921) Chinese Communist Party (CCP). While increased membership would provide the KMT with the broad popular support it sorely needed, the infusion of new blood only exacerbated a problem that had long plagued Sun – the matter of discipline and organization.

To overcome these weaknesses, Sun gradually turned to the Soviet Union and its Bolshevik leadership for assistance. Once again the West had angered him by refusing any substantial adjustment in the unequal treaty system at the Washington Conference (1921-1922). Inspired by Lenin's success in forging a new state system in Russia (a feat that owed much to the kind of party which he had created), impressed by the Soviet offer of assistance to China's revolution, and concerned with the growing influence of the Chinese Communist Party, Sun finally contacted the Soviet Union. In early 1923, after months of negotiations, he agreed to cooperate in the establishment of a United Front with the CCP in return for guidance from Soviet political and military advisers and financial backing. Making it clear that the Communists were entering the KMT and not vice-versa, he took steps to ensure that his new allies would not use the United Front to subvert the Nationalists or thoroughly communize their organization.

Still, Sun paid a price for the advisers, money, and weapons which now assisted his movement. On the one hand, they compelled him to modify the "Three People's Principles," which underlay the Nationalist program, to stress anti-imperialism, the need for strong government, and anti-capitalism, thereby bringing his previous pronouncements on nationalism, democracy, and the public welfare more in line with Soviet ideology. On the other hand, Sun created dissension within the ranks of the KMT because some of his followers refused to accept the party's reorientation. Despite his best efforts, many conservatives persisted in their disapproval of the United Front. When they came to dominate the party in 1927, they moved quickly to destroy the alliance.

• The Rise of Chiang Kai-shek and the Northern Campaign
(1926-1928)

Political reorganization along Bolshevik lines invigorated the KMT. Under the direction of Comintern agent Michael Borodin, Soviet advisers helped to centralize the party's administration, regularize its finances, and coordinate its propaganda. With Sun and his associates assuming effective leadership, Canton became the center of a small but enterprising government by 1925, a microcosm of Nationalist aspirations. Although recognized by neither warlords nor foreign powers, the Canton government rapidly consolidated itself and created its own "new model" army, which would provide the main force for the military effort to reunify China.

Following Sun Yat-sen's sudden death in March, 1925, in the midst of negotiations with the warlord faction at Peking, a struggle for control of the KMT ensued. One of the claimants was Chiang Kai-shek, a young military officer and director of the Whampoa Military Academy near Canton. Born in 1887 to a poor merchant family in Chekiang province, Chiang had met Sun in Japan and later participated in the revolutionary events of 1911-1912. For the next ten years, however, he generally remained aloof from politics. Not until 1923 did he emerge again as a devoted and active follower of Sun's cause. Nevertheless, within four years, he would become the leader of the KMT.

By 1926, the Canton government had grown strong enough to begin the long-awaited campaign against the northern warlords. Under Chiang's command, Nationalist forces swept into the Yangtze valley, overran half of China's provinces and "liberated" scores of important cities, often with the assistance of local Communist party cells. In the midst of the campaign, however, an open break occurred between conservative and radical wings of the KMT, fomented by Communist-inspired riots among the peasant and working classes and the killing of numerous foreigners. Both actions frightened the wealthier and more conservative members of the Kuomintang, the very people who were Chiang's principal supporters.

Suddenly, he attacked all Communist cells, following the capture of Shanghai. For a brief period, the political purge raged furiously, but by late March, 1927, the conservatives had triumphed with their resolve to sever the alliance with the Communists. By mid-April, they liquidated the Chinese radicals and dismissed the Russian advisers of the KMT, while survivors fled underground or to the safety of the countryside. Mao Tse-tung and Chu Teh, youthful leaders of the CCP, led two shattered contingents to the frontiers of Kiangsi, a southeastern province. Protected by its mountains and forests, they kept alive the Communist movement, regrouped its forces, and turned to guerrilla action against Chiang and his party, resolving to repay their "blood debt" to him for his betrayal of the alliance.

Meanwhile, his opposition crushed, Chiang resumed the Northern Campaign. By the end of 1928, his armies had occupied Peking and achieved at least nominal control over most of China. While many warlords continued to ignore his authority, the foreign powers recognized the new government which he established at Nanking. Financial assistance from abroad bolstered Chiang's regime, and tentative steps were taken toward a revision of the unequal treaties. Following the lead of the United States, the great powers agreed to relinquish control of the country's customs and tariffs, and over the next couple of years they abolished a number of foreign-held concessions. In such circumstances, there was every reason to expect that the victorious Kuomintang could now undertake the reconstruction of the country. Japanese aggression and the persistent opposition of the Communists, however, distracted Chiang's attention from this critical task.

## • The Japanese Invasion of Manchuria (1931-1933)

For Japan, the 1920s were a decade of growing crisis and disillusionment. All of the uncertainties engendered by modernization, coupled with population pressure and a weakening economy, worked together to create domestic tensions that ultimately would find release in foreign adventurism. Military leaders, alarmed by the worsening circumstances of Japanese rural life and resentful of their own lack of influence in determining their country's policies, began to maneuver for political power and to advocate a program of expansionism (beginning with China) as a cure for Japan's problems. They especially coveted the rich province of Manchuria. Convinced that Japan must directly control its raw materials vital to her industrial machine and great-power status, local officers in charge of the Japanese Kwangtung Army pressured for immediate action. On September 18, 1931, a minor explosion on the South Manchurian Railway near Mukden, set off by the Japanese but blamed on the Chinese, provided the pretext for a full-scale invasion of Manchuria. Meeting little resistance, the Japanese overran the entire region within five months. In doing so, they launched the long series of events that would lead to the Second World War.

At that time, Chiang Kai-shek chose not to fight because of China's weaknesses. In the southeast, his armies were still clashing with the Communists, whom he regarded as the more dangerous enemy. "The Japanese are a disease of the skin," he reportedly observed, "whereas the Communists are a disease of the heart." Resolved to avoid an armed clash with Japan and certain defeat, Chiang instead appealed to the League of Nations. He undoubtedly knew that this would be a vain effort, but he was seeking time to strengthen his hand. The League took up the issue, called for a cessation of hostilities, and sent an investigatory mission to the scene. Beyond this, however, it did nothing except express its moral disapproval of the Japanese, who by May, 1933, had successfully occupied China's four northeastern provinces. A truce signed at that time brought a temporary halt to Japanese expansion in China and acknowledged their acquisitions. Chiang felt justified in making concessions to avoid military disaster against the Japanese. As a result, the policy of "internal pacification before resistance to external aggression" continued to guide his actions. The decision to adopt this tactic, however, proved a costly miscalculation in the long run. Refusal to resist the Japanese eroded Chinese nationalism's support of Chiang, and his failure to capitalize on Japan's aggression lost a major opportunity to mobilize the Chinese people behind him.

## • The Nationalists and the Communists (1927-1937)

When the remnants of the Communist movement fled to Kiangsi following Chiang Kai-shek's attempt to liquidate it in 1927, the future looked bleak. Yet, by taking advantage of popular discontent to broaden its base of support, they created a professional military force (the Red Army) which refined the technique of guerrilla warfare into an effective strategy. Thus, the Communists were able to resist Chiang's armies successfully. While organizing a network of local cells, they established a Chinese Soviet Republic in the southeast by 1931 with Mao Tse-tung as the key figure.

Born in 1893, the son of a relatively well-to-do peasant family, Mao rebelled against landlordism and the tyranny of paternal authority at an early age. Like many youths during the first decades of the twentieth century, Mao was caught up in the groundswell of change and became a revolutionary activist. One of a handful of men responsible for founding the CCP in 1921, he assumed the task of organizing the peasants during the period of the United Front. His experiences in the countryside strengthened his conviction that the success of the Communist cause in China depended upon the mobilization of the peasantry. For years he argued this theoretical position long and hard against both Chinese and Russian Communist leaders, whose interpretation of Marxism-Leninism and infatuation with the Russian revolutionary experience led them to concentrate on the Chinese urban proletariat. But in the end he managed to convince the world of the rectitude of his contention that whoever won over the peasants would gain China.

Before that day arrived, however, Mao successfully parried Chiang Kai-shek's efforts to crush the Communist movement. Had Chiang been entirely free, he probably would have hounded the CCP remnants to extermination immediately following his 1927 purge. But other matters distracted him, thereby providing his archenemies a much-needed respite. Not until late in 1930 was he able to launch the first two "bandit annihilation offensives" designed to encircle the Communist stronghold in the Kiangsi-Hunan region. A rude surprise, however, awaited him. Rather than encountering a rag-tag force of disorganized rabble, Chiang's troops confronted well-trained, aggressive, and highly-mobile Red Army units which fought skillfully against a more numerous foe. The KMT suffered serious setbacks. In 1931, Chiang tried again, this time leading the attack himself. Success seemed imminent, but news of the Manchurian Incident forced a Nationalist withdrawal. Throughout the rest of the year and into 1932, Japanese aggression required most of Chiang's attention. After the situation in North China had stabilized somewhat, he conducted a fourth campaign against the Communists in late 1932 and 1933, but this ended in a stalemate. Advised by volunteer German officers, Chiang next constructed a series of blockhouses along the perimeter of the Communist-held territory. This relentlessly-tightening blockade would set the stage for the fifth KMT campaign, which by spring of 1934 was ready to deliver the final blow.

With the Nationalists closing in, the Communist leaders decided to abandon the base to escape strangulation. In October, 1934, the main force of some one hundred thousand men, women, and children slipped through the battlelines, headed west as far as the border of Tibet and then turned northward. Carrying all of their possessions, they crossed twenty-four rivers, eighteen mountain ranges, twelve separate provinces, and ten hostile warlord-held territories before completing what history would know as the

"Long March." After three hundred and sixty-eight days of flight over more than five thousand tortuous miles, walking mostly at night to escape Chiang's aircraft, only twenty thousand arrived at the final destination. Mao, who during the flight had succeeded in wresting leadership of the party from Stalin's agents or "returned students" (he was now chairman of the Politburo since the Tsunyi Conference of January, 1935), settled his force around Yenan, which would remain the Communists' headquarters until 1947, shortly before their final victory over the Nationalists.

The Long March, for all of its drama, had decimated the Communist ranks and thoroughly exhausted the survivors. Under those conditions, it seemed unlikely that they would be able to withstand the expected KMT attack on their new base. Chiang counted on Manchurian troops under the command of the "Young Marshal," Chang Hsüeh-liang, in his final battle with the Communists, but their commitment to an anti-Communist offensive took second place to a desire to liberate their homeland from Japanese occupation. When Chang Hsüeh-liang failed to move against Mao's forces as ordered, Chiang Kai-shek flew to Chang's headquarters at Sian in December, 1936. There he was confronted by rebellious officers who, encouraged by the Communists, demanded an end to the civil war and the formation of a United Front against the Japanese. Arrested and detained for two weeks, Chiang finally had to agree. As a result of the new alliance, following this Sian Incident, the Red Army was nominally placed under KMT command. In view of the fiasco of the first KMT-CCP cooperation in 1927, neither Mao nor Chiang had any illusions about the long-term success of the Second United Front. Nevertheless, for a short time most of China rallied behind Chiang in an outpouring of Nationalist sentiment that reflected a desire for all-out resistance to the Japanese.

## • China During the Sino-Japanese War (1937-1945)

Well before the Japanese launched their full-scale invasion of China in 1937, they had been making serious inroads in the country's northeastern sector and had engaged in extensive smuggling. Yet, when Chinese and Japanese troops clashed at the Marco Polo Bridge near Peiping (formerly Peking), on July 7, 1937, the Japanese did not expect or desire the incident to lead to all-out war. By this time, the Japanese military was headed by more responsible men than had been the case in the late 1920s, and Japan's goals were limited to consolidating her control over northern China so as to protect her interests from Russian interference. Had Chiang

Nationalist leader Chiang Kai-shek toasts Mao Tse-tung in Chunking (fall of 1945) in one of the failing attempts to create a coalition government with the Communists. United Press International.

Kai-shek followed his long-standing policy of negotiating with the Japanese and avoiding war, the events following the Marco Polo Bridge Incident might have taken a different course. But the Sian Incident and public objection to any further concessions or collaboration severely limited Chiang's options. While some negotiations were undertaken, growing hostility on both sides made accommodation impossible. The Japanese hoped to persuade Chiang to accede to their wishes by massing troops in the Peiping area and dispatching naval and military forces to take up positions off Shanghai. These moves, however, served only to deepen Japan's involvement in China and led to the outbreak of major hostilities at Shanghai on August 13, 1937. Although the belligerents did not make a legal declaration before December, 1941, the second Sino-Japanese War had begun.

The long years of fighting that would merge into World War II had ensued, despite the Japanese command's promise to the emperor that a mere two months' campaign would conquer northeastern China and terminate the conflict. Even though the Japanese eventually overran the great coastal cities and almost all of eastern China, thereby forcing the Nationalist government to transfer its capital far inland to Chungking, they had never planned to absorb the entire country. Safe behind the protective barriers of the upper Yangtze and the mountains of Szechuan, Chiang refused all peace offers while pressing for American entry into the conflict, tying down sizeable Japanese forces during World War II. Avoiding costly operations against the Japanese, because of Chinese military weaknesses, Chiang apparently reserved his resources for the day when he would resume action against the Communists, despite the counsel of American advisers.

But Chiang's prolonged refuge in his inland capital, in the end, did much to separate him from important segments of his people. Settled in Chungking, cut off from the industrial and banking resources of the coastal urban industrial centers, Chiang had to rely more and more on the conservative landlord class whose main goal was to preserve the old agrarian social system. In time the interests of this landlord group prevailed over the more progressive urban intellectual and business elements who had fled with the Nationalist government and who were more inclined to support necessary social and agrarian reform, antagonizing many of the latter elements from the KMT cause. In addition, evacuation of the eastern areas abandoned millions of peasants to brutal Japanese occupation, forcing many to turn away from the Nationalists and toward Communist guerrilla units for protection. Thus the Communists commenced their conquest of Chinese nationalism. Had Chiang proclaimed a future land reform program at the peak of his popularity (1938), he might have cemented peasant loyalty more effectively to his leadership.

Meanwhile, in Shensi province, the Communists were working to rebuild their shattered movement. Thanks to the declaration of the Second United Front and the Japanese invasion of China, they were relieved of serious military pressure throughout the years of the Sino-Japanese War. During that period, which began what is commonly called the "Yenan" stage of CCP history (from the fact that Yenan became the movement's northwest capital in January, 1937), a new revolutionary technique was born that would contribute to a remarkable reversal in the fortunes of the CCP and that continues to have political and psychological significance for Chinese Communists today. Lasting over a decade until 1947, the Yenan era also witnessed the consolidation of Mao's power within the party.

Perhaps most important, it was the period when Mao took up the study of Marxist-Leninist theory in earnest for the first time, evaluated it in the light of Chinese conditions, the experiences of the CCP over the previous two decades, and his own intellectual predispositions, and formulated a distinct variant of it known as "Maoism."

Maoism, of course, is first of all a method of political and social analysis. But it is also a set of concepts, an ideology, which provides the underlying motive for action. Complex and diffuse, the "thoughts of Mao Tse-tung" can be defined, however, by a few basic precepts. First, Maoism promoted the idea that human consciousness is the decisive factor in history and that men's wills and actions can not only change objective reality but also accomplish the seemingly impossible. Second, Maoism emphasizes the development and maintenance of "correct" thought in order to be able to analyze properly current situations and conditions so as to be prepared to take advantage of immediate opportunities for revolutionary action. As a result, Maoists have refused to be restricted by the rigid formulas of Marxism-Leninism as proclaimed by Moscow, and instead have granted more importance to "subjective factors" in the determination of strategy and tactics. Third, Maoism argues for the distinctiveness of the Chinese revolution and, conversely, for the limited applicability of the Russian experience as a model for China. "Although we must value Soviet experience," Mao wrote in 1936, "and even value it somewhat more than experiences in other countries throughout history, . . . we must value even more the experience of China's revolutionary war, because there are a great number of conditions special to the Chinese revolution and the Chinese Red Army." What determined China's uniqueness in Mao's opinion were three characteristics: (1) she was a semi-colonial country; (2) she was controlled not by one but by several imperialist powers; and (3) economically and politically she was "unevenly" developed. From these observations Mao drew two conclusions: first, that the very uniqueness of China's situation made the likelihood of a successful revolution there even greater; and second, that the revolution would spread from the rural areas to engulf the semimodern and nonrevolutionary cities.

The Yenan experience entailed, however, more than just the development of the ideology which would lead the CCP and its supporters to victory by 1949. On the practical side, it was characterized by the abandonment of the United Front with the Nationalists in early 1942 and its replacement by a commitment to build a unified party on Maoist foundations. The "rectification" (*cheng-feng*) movement of 1942-1944 sought to bring an end to party heterodoxy and to instill in cadres common ideology and goals. Through intense criticism and self-criticism and the study of selected documents clearly in line with Mao's views, thousands of party members (many of them recent recruits) were introduced to "correct" thought and made more amenable to accept the radical shift in policy which the party was about to initiate.

By 1941, the failure of the United Front strategy and severe losses to the Japanese had revealed shortcomings in prevailing CCP policies and tactics. As a consequence, the party leadership, headed by Mao, devised a new strategy to sustain the movement, prevent further erosion of support, and ultimately to strengthen the whole Communist cause and prepare it for the next round of action. The rectification campaign was an essential step in that direction, but it was accompanied by a number of other campaigns, moderate in spirit, yet designed to indoctrinate the people, exclude as few as possible from the revolutionary process, unleash the energies of the masses, and direct them toward the task of solving social problems in the Communist-held base areas. Among the many programs inaugurated in those years were: (1) the "to the village" campaign (1941 and 1942), which helped to break down the isolation of many communities by sending cadres into their midst and shifting the focus of government work to the lower levels of society; (2) the campaign for the reduction of rents and interest (1942-1944), which served to awaken apathetic peasants by rallying them around an issue that had great appeal; (3) the cooperative movement (1942-1944), which, by stressing the concept of mutual aid, worked to increase production and develop new relationships among peasants; and (4) the education movement of 1944, which spread literacy and indoctrinated the masses in Communist ideology. It is instructive that the party's emphasis was on adult education rather than that of children during this campaign.

Through programs such as these, the party sought to mobilize the masses, involve them actively in resolving the many problems which beset them, and gain their commitment to the Communist cause by seemingly equating its goals with theirs. The success of the campaigns, however, depended on the effectiveness of mobilization. To encourage and increase popular involvement, the party developed a propaganda technique known as the "mass line." Simple and not very original in concept, the technique comprised a three-stage process. First, cadres would go to the people to determine what kind of program appealed to them. Once the determination had been made, the second step was to square popular desires with party ideology and goals. This was often the most difficult task because in the third stage the cadres had to persuade the masses that to support the program was in their best interests. Even more than that, the key to the success of the mass line technique was in arousing the people to believe in the program and to act upon it with true commitment. The mass line opened up leadership possibilities for peasants through its promotion of quasi-democratic debate; it also provided the needed link between the party and the masses to involve every individual in the effort to resist the Japanese and to reconstruct the economy and restructure the political and social order within the base areas. As a leadership technique, the mass line has become a permanent feature of the Chinese Communist scene.

The results of the campaigns of the early 1940s and use of the mass line technique had scored by the end of the Sino-Japanese War in 1945. Communist propaganda reached millions of people, party membership had risen to 1.2 million (compared with 40,000 in 1937), and the Red Army numbered about one million men. What had been a movement on the verge of extinction only ten years before was now capable of challenging the KMT for the leadership of China. It not only had developed the material resources, the organizational ability, and the military tactics to succeed, but more importantly had the support of millions indoctrinated with Communist ideals and a feeling of confidence in the struggle's outcome.

## • U.S. Assistance and the Stilwell Controversy (1940-1944)

As Nationalist allegiance in the provinces steadily weakened, Chiang's regime at Chungking grew increasingly isolated, unable to take much part in the war against Japan after Pearl Harbor. In 1940, the Japanese established a puppet government at Nanking under his old enemy, Wang Ching-wei. Chiang's coalition with the Communists collapsed after a Communist-Nationalist clash on the lower Yangtze in January, 1941, and from then on, his army clamped a tight blockade (excluding all trade) on the Communist areas. The Chinese civil war resumed from that point.

In addition, Chiang's relations with his foreign allies came under considerable stress as they found it increasingly difficult to assist him. U.S. and British aid dated from 1931, the Russian from 1937. But the Japanese conquest of Southeast Asia (1941-1942) isolated Chungking. Flights over the Himalayas ("the Hump") brought some U.S. help just as Russian arms shipments through Sinkiang came to a halt. In the words of General George C. Marshall, the U.S. Army Chief of Staff, China was "at the end of the thinnest supply line of all." The "Europe First" strategy of the allied powers also put China far down on the priority list — "like feeding an elephant with an eye dropper." President Franklin D. Roosevelt, however, wanted Nationalist China to participate actively in the war in order to replace Japan in the future East Asian power balance. Washington projected an invasion of Burma to secure access to Chungking, and the president appointed General Joseph W. Stilwell as Chiang's chief of staff for the newly-created China-Burma-India theater. Born in 1883, Stilwell graduated from West Point and saw extensive duty in the Far East where he became fluent in Mandarin Chinese.

In the early 1920s he headed a language school in Peking under General Marshall. Although Stilwell personally trained a Chinese army for the campaign, the Japanese disastrously defeated his first Burma invasion in 1942.

Stilwell proposed drastic reforms for the Nationalist army: reduction to a smaller, more efficient size, elimination of the warlord element, and full cooperation with the Communists. Mao Tse-tung's mobile guerrilla warfare against the Japanese dominated the countryside in many occupied regions. Communist leaders offered to place their forces under Stilwell's command when the general journeyed to Yenan for talks. Stilwell then tried to persuade Chiang to reach an agreement with Mao and to withdraw his blockade of Communist areas.

Chiang procrastinated, as he secretly did not share these views. He could not directly oppose Stilwell's reform program, however, lest this jeopardize American aid. Yet he realized that reduction of the army would eliminate his landlord support, while a modernized force might defect to the Communists. Moreover, Chiang deeply distrusted the Yenan proposal since two agreements already had been shattered. Gradually, Stilwell discerned Chiang's attitude. Despite a successful Burma campaign in 1943, the American quarreled constantly with the Chinese leader. When President Roosevelt proposed Stilwell for commander in chief of the Nationalist forces in 1944, Chiang resented this intrusion on his authority and demanded Stilwell's recall. When the general returned to the United States, he expressed his bitterness to the news media. Stilwell's subsequent discussions with General Marshall undoubtedly dimmed the latter's view of the China situation prior to the Marshall Mission in 1945-1947.

Stilwell's criticism of Chiang's regime exposed much of its so-called "corruption" to the American people, who hitherto had regarded Chiang as an heroic figure. The erosion of American support for the Generalissimo began from that point.

● **The Civil War (1945-1949)**

The Far Eastern extension of the Second World War came to an end in August, 1945, but in its wake peace did not come to China. No sooner had the Japanese capitulation been announced than both Communist and Nationalist forces rushed to fill the vacuum created by their departing enemy and secure control of as much of China as possible. In the scramble for territory, the advantage seemed to lie with the Nationalists. For one thing, the Japanese had been ordered to surrender only to Chiang Kai-shek's forces; for another, American ships and planes facilitated the movement of Nationalist troops from their inland positions to the coastal areas and northern China. At this point, however, Chiang made two major tactical blunders that significantly affected the outcome of the civil war. The first was his decision to concentrate on the occupation of the principal cities. While not a surprising move on his part, in view of the KMT's long-standing reliance on China's urban economy and population, it was militarily disastrous because it allowed the Communists to gain firm control of the countryside. The second error resulted from Chiang's decision to commit some of his best divisions to Manchuria, trying to prevent division of the country north and south. He hoped to seize this industrial region and strike a crippling blow against the Communists; instead, he found out very quickly that his lines of communications and supply were stretched dangerously thin, extremely vulnerable to the guerrilla tactics used so effectively by the Red Army. Also the Russians had thoroughly looted the province and then presented stored Japanese arms to the Chinese Communists as they entered Manchuria.

Meanwhile, American efforts to mediate KMT-CCP differences in the hopes of avoiding a full scale civil war continued. In December, 1945, President Harry S. Truman sent General Marshall to China to negotiate with Communists and Nationalists alike. As a result of a Political Consultative Conference attended by delegates from both camps, Marshall was able to announce several agreements that held out promise for a peaceful resolution of China's potentially explosive political troubles. The Conference called for a military truce to begin immediately, established procedures for moving China in the direction of a political settlement that would be democratic in nature, and envisioned the eventual integration of Communist and Nationalist armies into a non-politicized national military force.

The spirit of compromise proved ephemeral. Almost immediately, disputes over the political control of certain areas, notably Manchuria, led to military clashes. The violations of the truce reported by American officers mounted through the remainder of 1946. Communist complaints were directed not only at the refusal of some Nationalist commanders to honor the truce but also at the KMT government for its clear lack of commitment to the proposed establishment of a constitutional order in China. Moreover, as mediator, Marshall found his neutral position compromised because the United States openly supported one of the belligerents. By the beginning of 1947, his last effort to reconcile the country's contending forces proved an obvious failure, and both KMT and CCP leaders prepared their supporters for all-out civil war to determine the future leadership of China.

The outcome of the struggle still could not be determined as late as 1947. In that year the Nationalists launched a major offensive that resulted in some dramatic victories (such as the capture of Yenan, the Communist capital); yet, such triumphs as were claimed by Chiang Kai-shek had very little substance and did nothing to either strengthen his position or weaken that of the Communists. By the spring of 1948, in fact, Red Army tactics of avoiding major clashes with KMT troops in favor of harassment of supply lines and encirclement of Nationalist-held cities had begun to tip the balance in its favor. A major Communist success was achieved in Manchuria where Chiang's forces had isolated themselves and had taken up defensive positions in and around the major urban centers. Denied the opportunity to either attack or withdraw, KMT troops found themselves caught in numerous traps, cut off and surrounded. By the summer of 1948, Red Army units had succeeded in completely severing overland supply lines to Manchuria, with the result that Nationalist troops had to be provisioned by air. From summer through late autumn, the KMT military situation deteriorated rapidly. Heavy troop losses following the evacuation of several Manchurian cities and the surrender of the army at Mukden were accompanied by the abandonment of huge amounts of American supplies and armaments which then fell into the eager hands of the Communists. By December, China north of the Yangtze was under Red Army control and Nationalist resistance had been all but shattered. James E. Sheridan, the American historian, offered a graphic illustration of the victorious Communist guerrilla strategy. He compared the Chinese landscape to a checkerboard, wherein Mao's forces in the rural areas occupied the spaces, while his Japanese and Nationalist opponents controlled the lines (the roads, railways, and communications), and especially the intersecting points, where the cities were located. Thus, Mao utilized domination of the countryside to surround and strangle the enemy.

Defeated on the field of battle, hamstrung by economic collapse, panicked by runaway inflation (the *yüan*-to-dollar exchange rate had risen from 1,000 to 1 in 1945 to 45,000 to 1 in mid-1947) and cancerous fiscal corruption, unable to maintain the morale of its supporters, and abandoned by millions who felt that their interests had been too long ignored, the Nationalist government faced a situation that few would have thought possible even five years before. In one last desperate ploy to salvage at least something of KMT influence in Chinese affairs, Chiang resigned the presidency and sought a negotiated settlement with his adversary. The time for such maneuvers, however, was long past. Flushed with their victories in the north, the Communists used the negotiations to consolidate their hold over territory already acquired and prepare for the anticipated campaign to "liberate" China south of the Yangtze. In 1949, the final push commenced, meeting only token resistance as one after another of the great cities — Nanking, Shanghai, and Canton — fell. Meanwhile, with most of his government, some 50,000 troops, and two and a half million civilians, Chiang Kai-shek withdrew to the island of Taiwan. The civil war was over, but many aspects of the China problem remained.

- ## Epilogue: The Nationalists on Taiwan (1949-1978)

Chiang's evacuation of the mainland in December, 1949, brought millions of refugees to the island of Taiwan (the Portuguese called it Formosa, "Beautiful Island"). These recent arrivals soon controlled the central government, while native Taiwanese, who were descendants of seventeenth-century Chinese immigrants, ran the local administration. One of Chiang's first measures was to inaugurate land reform by reducing rents to thirty-seven and one-half percent of produce and encouraging more peasant ownership. United States foreign aid (about three billion dollars' worth over fifteen years) spurred the economy so successfully that assistance halted in 1965. Since that date, the island's GNP has increased ten percent yearly, and foreign trade has grown annually by twenty-five percent. Taiwan's achievements during the past decade markedly resemble Japan's "economic miracle" over much of the same period.

American, European, and especially Japanese investments poured into the island. Japan took advantage of the cheap labor Taiwan had to offer, only twenty-five percent of her own costs, to establish automobile, electronics, and textile factories. Many Japanese firms sent units to Taiwan

A view of the East Gate of the city of Taipei, capital of the Republic of China on Taiwan. Chinese Information Service.

for pre-assembly prior to completion at home. The Japanese remembered that in 1945 Chiang had advised other allied leaders to retain Japan's emperor, had promptly returned one million Japanese prisoners, and had foresworn reparations following World War II.

Taiwan's industrial growth accelerated after October, 1971, despite the United Nations' expulsion of Nationalist China. Although many countries broke diplomatic relations in order to recognize Peking, Chiang's government pushed ahead with economic expansion in an attempt to become commercially indispensable to the outside world — a "Switzerland of the Far East" or perhaps an "Israel of Asia." Overseas trade increased an amazing forty percent annually for each of the three years following the ouster. Hastily-withdrawn investments soon returned from abroad.

The Republic of China on Taiwan presents an admirable post-war economic success story — a showcase of national development for the

Third World. Although he failed on the mainland, Chiang's success on Taiwan did much to mitigate previous errors of judgment and acted as his fitting memorial in April, 1975, when he died at age eighty-seven. His son, Premier Chiang Ching-kuo, succeeded him as effective head of state. Despite her remarkable technological progress, the Nationalist regime still faced an uncertain future, but with courage and resolution. The Communist government of the People's Republic of China on the mainland insisted that the United States sever all links with Taiwan and agree to complete evacuation of their troops as Peking's price for full diplomatic relations with the Americans. Recalling that her Taiwan trade was eight times her commerce with the mainland, the U.S. requested a repudiation of the use of Communist force. The presence of a huge Soviet army on the northern Chinese frontier, along with an obvious deficiency in Communist amphibious invasion facilities, as well as the efficiency and political broadening of the Kuomintang government, however, ensured the continued existence of the Nationalist regime. When the retirement of President Yen Chia-kan occurred in early spring of 1978, Chiang Ching-kuo moved finally into his father's old position.

# 4

# *Communist Revolution to the Present (1949-1978)*

MAO TSE-TUNG PROCLAIMED the People's Republic of China (PRC) on October 1, 1949, before cheering millions in Peking's famous T'ien-an-men Square. This was one of the great turning points in recent world history, for it inaugurated an attempt to transform China and her people that has continued ever since. If the goal of constructing a new China has gone virtually unchallenged since 1949, the means for its achievement have not been so easily agreed upon. Much of the history of the People's Republic over the past quarter century has been determined by shifts in policy that have derived from an on-going dispute over one fundamental question: Is the "revolution" over? That is, is it necessary to continue the effort to transform the character of the Chinese people, or can the elite and society turn to the task of developing the material base of the country? This question, despite its apparent simplicity, in fact encompasses others which have defined the main parameters of factionalism in Chinese politics: What role should ideology play in China's development? What should be the nature and goals of policy? By what means should policy be implemented? To understand the internal and external developments of the People's Republic since 1949 requires that one focus upon these issues and the tensions and conflicts which they have fostered. In doing so, it will become clear that the path from 1949 to the present has been neither straight nor smooth for China.

Like all revolutionaries, who spend years in the struggle to win power, the Chinese Communists before 1949 devoted little attention to specific policies that they would pursue after attaining victory. Concerned more with the survival and expansion of the revolutionary movement, Mao and his colleagues gave little consideration to the future. As a result, when the "future" arrived at mid-century, the CCP was suddenly faced with all of the responsibilities that come with wielding power as well as the pressing need to undertake two major tasks: the reintegration of political authority after nearly four decades of ineffective central control over all of China; and the reconstruction of an economy shattered by years of civil and international strife.

## • Recovery and Consolidation (1949-1952)

In spite of the mood of optimism which permeated the ranks of the CCP in 1949, the wide popular support which the party enjoyed, and the dedication and discipline which the rank-and-file would bring to the tasks at hand, the new regime had to proceed slowly and with moderation over the next several years. Mao understood this perfectly and pointed out repeatedly that China was not yet prepared for the "second revolution" intended to transform her thoroughly. Socialist construction, the first stage in this process, would have to await the political and economic stabilization of the country.

Given the limited numbers and inadequate training of party cadres, success in achieving the goals of rehabilitating the country and consolidating the new regime came to depend in part on the party's ability to approach China's problems with ideological flexibility and moderation. The conscious decision to de-emphasize theoretical considerations for more pragmatic goals enabled the party to mobilize all available human resources, accept temporary solutions, and retain many of the old Nationalist administrators. Along with ideological temporizing, the party worked to organize the population, much as it had done on a lesser scale during the Yenan period, in order to achieve major political and/or social change with full mass participation. Between 1950 and 1953 party cadres launched several movements which left hardly any of China's millions untouched: (1) the land reform movement (1950-1952), conducted to involve the rural masses in peasant associations and "people's courts" for the purposes of completing the process of breaking up large landholdings, equalizing the distribution of land among farm owners and laborers, and undercutting the traditional power of the landlord class; (2) the campaign for "implementation of the marriage law" (beginning in 1950), designed to end the inequality of Chinese women (epitomized and maintained by the traditional marriage system) and involve them in public activity of all kinds; (3) the "Resist America-Aid Korea" campaign (1950-1953), begun to intensify patriotic sentiment and recruit volunteers for the army in support of Chinese participation in the Korean War; (4) the "thought reform" campaigns (1950 and after), organized to attack traditional and "bourgeois" ideas and values through programs of self-evaluation, mutual criticism, and indoctrination; (5) the "bandit suppression" campaigns (1951), inaugurated to root out remnants of active Nationalist resistance and persons suspected of inadequate loyalty to the new regime; (6) the "three-anti" campaign (1951-1952), initiated to rectify the behavior of party cadres and government officials who were accused of corruption, waste, and bureaucratism; and (7) the "five-anti" campaign (1951-1952), directed largely at urban middle-class businessmen for their alleged "bribery, tax evasion, theft of state assets, cheating on government contracts, and stealing of state economic secrets."

The success of these separate campaigns varied, as did their impact on individual Chinese. But from the standpoint of the CCP, the gains acquired through these efforts at mass mobilization (and through adoption of conciliatory policies) were significant. By 1953, not only was the economy revived, state control over it increased, and the political system strengthened, but society was also organized to a degree that seemed to prove China's readiness for the transition to socialism.

## • The First Five Year Plan (1953-1957)

In late 1952, the Chinese leadership announced the First Five Year Plan (FFYP) for the following year, although it was not put into full practice until February, 1955. Designed to rapidly move the country forward economically, it had all the earmarks of Soviet Russian influence: emphasis on industry rather than agriculture, heavy industry rather than light, large enterprises rather than small, centralized planning, and full exploitation of the peasantry through collectivization in order to finance development. To accompany the plan and assist its fulfillment, technical and monetary aid flowed from the USSR, the population was mobilized to increase production, moderation prevailed in political life (as did institutionalization), and a policy of "peaceful coexistence" and renewed contact with the outside world characterized China's foreign relations. In sum, at least until 1956, the general thrust of party policies was in the direction of minimizing social and political tensions so as to avoid disrupting production and proceed with the task of nation-building.

The successes of the First Five Year Plan were reward enough for the immense commitment of resources. Agriculture, although underfunded, seemed to be thriving — the summer of 1955 provided the best crop since 1949 — and practically all peasant households had been collectivized (although not without growing peasant objection). As for industrial development, gains were even more impressive. For some within the Chinese leadership, however, there were disturbing aspects of the FFYP. As a result, an intense debate within the party ensued in 1956-1957 over the implications of FFYP results and trends. The opponents, who have been called pragmatists or conservatives on the one side, and idealists or radicals on the other, found themselves at odds over issues of policy and ideology. (It should be emphasized, however, that at this time the distinctions between positions were not yet hard and fast.) Specifically, several concerns sparked the debate. First, should priority continue to be given to industrial development (that is, should economic growth be "uneven" between industry and agriculture)? Second, should the socialization, even communization, of the countryside continue regardless of the potentially disruptive effect it might have on the economy? In other words, should economic development continue to receive higher priority than social revolution? Third, should the bureaucratization of Chinese administrative practice and planning be allowed to proceed unchecked because it was "necessary" for the kind of rapid economic development implied by the FFYP? Fourth, should the revolution be institutionalized instead of perpetuated (that is, should greater emphasis be placed on establishment of regular procedures and institutions so as to provide the needed social stability for orderly national growth, or on the notions of social struggle and "contradictions among peoples" and the practice of mass mobilization)? Fifth, should the party continue to rule unopposed? Regardless of one's position on these issues, the FFYP offered ammunition which could be used against one's opponents. The conservatives could point to solid evidence of growth and the potential for continued growth if only realism would prevail among China's decision-makers; as for the radicals, they could point to the threat to the revolution posed by bureaucratization, institutionalization, centralization, and excessive pragmatism.

As the leader in the latter "camp," Mao felt compelled to intervene directly and use his enormous prestige to challenge the thinking of the pragmatists, modify the FFYP, and "correct" some of the worst tendencies emerging from it. He was driven to this course of action not only by domestic Chinese concerns but by events within the Soviet Union and Eastern Europe: specifically, Premier Nikita S. Khrushchev's denunciation in February, 1956, of Stalinism and the uprising in Hungary from late October to early November of the same year.

At first Mao appears to have been unsuccessful, since it now seems clear that his opponents, led by Liu Shao-ch'i, a revolutionary comrade of Mao's since 1921, had enough support in the party and governmental apparatus to temper and control the radicals and their policies. This was certainly the case with regard to the countryside, where the collectivization process continued but was slowed, steps were taken to make it less disruptive of traditional rural village organization, and the peasants were restored the right to maintain private plots and livestock. Pragmatist domination of the ruling organs was also reflected in the public assertion of collective leadership within the party, a concept which, inspired by Khrushchev's critique of Stalin's "cult of personality" directly challenged Mao's authority. Mao continued to defend his positions in private and public, with articles in the press and speeches (notably his "On the Correct Handling of Contradictions among the People," delivered in February, 1957), and most dramatically by means of the "Hundred Flowers" campaign (May-June, 1957), which invited people in and out of the party to speak their minds about the state of the country and the CCP leadership. The volume and range of criticism, however, surprised all of China's leaders, including Mao. The party's response was to close the door immediately and launch "anti-rightist" and rectification campaigns to root out erroneous and counter-revolutionary tendencies among elite groups and expand socialist education (ideological training) among the masses. In addition, party leaders, only recently opposing one another, agreed to seek accommodation, gloss over their differences, and present a united front against a society which was obviously not yet imbued with the revolutionary spirit needed to build Communism in China. Maintaining the party's political hegemony was unquestioned, not only in light of the "weeds" which had sprouted during the "Hundred Flowers" campaign but also the counter-revolutionary character of the Hungarian uprising some months earlier.

The temporary healing of party wounds seems to have benefitted Mao the most. He had been losing ground to his opponents, but now had managed not only to save face but to rally sufficient support to enable him to impress his views on the economic and political decisions that would affect China for the next couple of years. The set of policies that began to emerge with the convening of the Third Plenum of the Central Committee in September-October, 1957, were to acquire the designation of "Great Leap Forward."

## • The Great Leap Forward (1957-1960)

The Great Leap Forward (GLF), which coincided roughly with the inauguration of the Second Five Year Plan but gradually subsumed it, was less a program of specific measures (although these were issued) than a set of ideological assumptions. These endeavored to establish a frame of mind that would make possible a frantic drive to harness the total energies of the Chinese people for the task of propelling the country into the future. The assumptions, not necessarily novel but certainly expressed with extraordinary vigor and fanaticism, were three in number. One was a commitment to the concept of voluntarism; that is, to the idea that the human will can accomplish the impossible and can be a decisive factor in history. Another was contained in the slogan "Politics takes command," which implied that China's problems and her very backwardness were less matters of economics than politics. Ultimately, "correct" politics and "proper" thinking would be more important than investment capital, fertilizer, or technical expertise, and one's political reliability ("redness") would count for more than one's specialized skills. The third cornerstone of the GLF was the belief in the possibility and necessity of simultaneously developing all areas of Chinese life. To give priority to some spheres would only delay the arrival of full Communism as other aspects lagged behind.

The reasons for fostering the GLF mentality were probably numerous, but they all come back to a basic dilemma facing the CCP leadership. During the First Five Year Plan, investment in heavy industry consumed roughly one-half of Chinese capital with perhaps another ten percent going to light industry. Total industrial production grew by about 140 percent as a result, thereby justifying the large investment. Agriculture, however, which was to help finance further industrial growth through surplus production, was able to increase output during the same period only enough to provide for China's expanding population. Failure to raise agricultural production in 1956 and 1957 only added to the problem, as did declining peasant willingness to continue making the sacrifices demanded of them. As a result, the party found itself faced with a major dilemma: how to win over the masses to the effort of increasing agricultural production, while at the same time continuing the rapid industrialization of China without adequate investment resources?

The solution was to exploit to the fullest China's massive population, to do with people what was otherwise impossible. Hence the Great Leap Forward (GLF) began, with its emphasis on mass line and mass mobilization, socialist education, economic decentralization (epitomized by the backyard furnaces which sprang up by the thousands to produce steel), competition and quotas rising to extraordinary heights, a foreign policy that encouraged belief in China as a beleaguered nation, and especially the reorganization of rural life into communes. All of these facets of the GLF phenomenon were viewed as means for turning liabilities into assets and weaknesses into strengths. Above all, it was thought that they would lead not only to economic progress but also to the creation of a new society by breaking down traditional barriers between city and countryside, industry and agriculture, intellectual and physical labor.

Begun in late 1957, the GLF was in trouble well before the end of 1958. To be sure there were positive results that could be counted (or at least official reports of such). Production of many commodities probably did increase, even dramatically in some cases, as a consequence of mobilizing the country's manpower as never before and encouraging the kind of feverish labor reminiscent of Stalin's Five Year Plans in Soviet Russia during the mid and late 1930s. The positive results, however, were easily overshadowed by the failures and the damage done to agriculture and industry. The GLF simply did not work, whether owing to adverse weather conditions and party cadre failings, as claimed by Mao, or the irrationality of the Great Leap concept itself and the resistance of the peasantry to communization and regimentation, as argued by many Western specialists. Rather than advancing the economy, the GLF nearly wrecked it; and rather than leading China to some golden age, it only engendered crisis. Moreover, the unity which had characterized the party leadership in the autumn of 1957 was now dissipated, and the differences of opinion over policy now re-emerged to coalesce into several factions which would engage in a power struggle for most of the next decade. The announcement of Mao's replacement by Liu Shao-ch'i as head of state in April, 1959, given little attention at the time, was in fact one of the first signs of the political crisis underway.

As criticism of the GLF grew, numerous conferences were held in 1958 and early 1959, during which Great Leap policies came under increased attack. Toward the summer of 1959, Mao attempted to counter his opponents and salvage the GLF. He succeeded temporarily when the Eighth Plenum of the Central Committee (July-August) called for a campaign against rightists (that is, Mao's opponents), reasserted the correctness of GLF policies, and forced the dismissal of Defense Minister P'eng Teh-huai, the critics' leading spokesman. Mao's victory, however, was shortlived. By the end of 1960 his influence had once again declined as more discouraging and negative news concerning the economy poured in. By the time the Ninth Plenum of the Central Committee met in

January, 1961, the pragmatists had succeeded in wresting control of the party and rejecting the Great Leap approach.

## • From Recovery and Retrenchment to Cultural Revolution (1961-1969)

Concerning domestic matters, the years from 1961 to 1965 witnessed two concurrent developments. On the one hand, with the reins of party and government firmly in their grasp, the pragmatists under Liu Shao-ch'i devoted their attention to economic restoration and political retrenchment. In order to revive the economy, measures were taken to centralize planning once again, increase the production of consumer goods, establish incentives for the peasants (including permission to use private plots and organize free markets), emphasize expertise rather than "redness," and de-radicalize the communes by reorganizing them and limiting their size. In the political sphere, along with efforts to play down mass mobilization and socialist education, the Liuists purged the middle and lower level party organs and replaced Maoist cadres with their own supporters and "experts." Veiled attacks against the Great Leap and Mao's leadership multiplied, including that contained in a soon-to-be-famous play produced in 1961 entitled *Hai-Jui Dismissed From Office.* Taken together, the economic and political policies of Liu and his colleagues provided the means for recovering from the extreme disruption of the Great Leap period and represented a desire to give priority to economic over political matters.

Meanwhile, those same years witnessed a persistent, initially low-keyed effort by Mao to win back his former influence over the CCP. Unhappy with his own political demise and the current "line" of the pragmatists, and convinced that the Great Leap was a sound approach to solving China's problems, he campaigned to win new supporters and to lay the foundation of yet another attempt both to rectify the party and change the thought and behavior of the Chinese people. Finding himself without a sufficient audience in the central organizations of the party and government, Mao turned to local and provincial cadres (notably in Shanghai) for allies. He also engaged the services of the army through his protégé Lin Piao, named Defense Minister after P'eng Teh-huai's dismissal in 1958. Finally, as the struggle for power came increasingly into the open, Mao appealed to China's youth to rally to his cause. With these allies, he launched a nationwide campaign known as the Great Proletarian Cultural Revolution (GPCR) in 1966. The battle was joined — "Red vs. Expert."

What was the GPCR? It probably defies full explanation, although one thing is now certain: it was the result of long-standing conflicts among party leaders over power, ideology, and policy, which until the mid-1960s had remained largely hidden from the outside world. One of the most surprising features of a phenomenon filled with startling and bizarre events was Mao's apparent willingness to risk the destruction of the very party which he had spent so many years nurturing and trying to shape. In his view, the CCP had become a haven for rightists and "capitalist-roaders," and having lost touch with the masses, had betrayed the revolution as a result. Since the party was dominated by men who would not accept Mao's views, he had no choice but to strike out at the country's leading institution. His weapons were propaganda against his opponents and in favor of his own positions (hence the enormous emphasis on the "Little Red Book" and the "thoughts of Mao"), and a politicized army and youth. The army, in fact, was increasingly portrayed as a model for society, and students and other young people were formed into units of Red Guards. As the GPCR unfolded, demands for rectification of the party were accompanied by an extraordinary effort to change the content of literature, art, and the theater (in this work Mao's wife, Chiang Ch'ing, was prominent), reform the educational system, and reject the values and attitudes of traditional China, all in the name of some vague "proletarian" virtues and orientation. Mao's goal was to preserve for and transmit to the rising generation the revolutionary spirit which it had never experienced.

The course of the Cultural Revolution is too complex to be dealt with here in any detail. It should be noted, however, that Mao's tactic was to isolate his major enemies and tarnish their names by attacking directly their subordinates and/or persons known to be associated with them. This he did successfully early on with P'eng Chen, Peking's mayor, later with Teng Hsiao-ping, the party secretary-general, and ultimately with Liu Shao-ch'i himself. At the Eleventh Plenum of the Central Committee (August 1-12, 1966), Mao's forces succeeded in winning control of that body and issuing in its name a "Sixteen-Point Decision" which officially sanctioned the Cultural Revolution. Thereafter the GPCR escalated and spread throughout the country, bringing with it a tidal wave of unrest, economic and political disruption, and near civil war. By the time that revolutionary committees had been set up nationwide in September, 1968, Mao, probably under the calming influence of Premier Chou En-lai, had begun the process of restoring order, phasing out the activities of the Red Guards, and consolidating the changes that had occurred in Chinese life. His victory seemingly won, his enemies purged from positions of authority, and his vision of the new China in everyone's mind, Mao could now pause in his race to the future to rebuild the party and the economy which lay in rubble about him.

## • Foreign Relations

Since 1949 China's foreign relations have undergone a series of bewildering changes that have seen *détente* (relaxation of tensions) with "imperialistic" America, considerable accommodation with the former Japanese enemy, and virtually total alienation from her revolutionary ally, the Soviet Union.

U.S. support of Nationalist China antagonized Mao towards Americans despite efforts by their consular officials (remaining behind in the larger cities in 1949) to open negotiations with the victorious Communists. Ambassador John Leighton Stuart talked with the Communist representative, Huang Hua (a former student), with no success. During the Korean War (1950-1953), the commitment of the U.S. Seventh Fleet to the protection of Taiwan and China's eventual intrusion into the conflict finally created an implacable enmity towards the United States for the next two decades.

Despite occasional talks in Warsaw with Chinese Communists, the U.S. agreed to defend the Nationalists on Taiwan by the Treaty of 1954 and thereafter successfully maneuvered to prevent admission of the People's Republic to the United Nations. When Peking attempted to seize the offshore islands in the Taiwan Strait (1958-1959), President Dwight D. Eisenhower threatened retaliation. The "running sore" of Vietnam brought war close by, as this former T'ang outlying dependency had served as a buffer, protecting China's southeastern frontier. Following the Communist victory over the French in Indo-China, the Geneva Treaty of 1954 had divided Vietnam into northern and southern zones, the latter with a U.S.-sponsored government. When Communist North Vietnam infiltrated southward, the United States sent military advisers to Saigon's forces. In 1964, the president introduced combat units and commenced restricted air strikes the following year. Despite a U.S. pledge not to invade North Vietnam, China felt endangered, recalling her experiences with "foreign devils" in the nineteenth century.

The United States struggled in quicksand, unable to advance or withdraw, as "protracted war" bled her forces in Vietnam. The fighting soon spread to Laos and Cambodia, engulfing all of Indo-China. Skillfully

President Chiang Ching-kuo was formerly premier of the Republic of China on Taiwan. Chung Hwa Information Service.

exploiting the Sino-Soviet split, however, U.S. Secretary of State Henry A. Kissinger negotiated a treaty facilitating American withdrawal in February, 1973 — part of the new *détente* policy with both China and the U.S.S.R. The United Nations' admission of the People's Republic to full membership in October, 1971, and President Richard M. Nixon's trip to Peking the following year had provided effective diplomatic preparation.

Some American difficulties with China remained, however. The Chinese government still insisted on the return of Taiwan and maintained a deep concern for Washington's commitments to the U.S.S.R. These differences made for a rather cool reception of President Gerald R. Ford and Secretary Kissinger on the occasion of their visit in December, 1975. Despite this momentary downturn in relations, however, China still sought an American presence in East Asia as a force for stability — especially to balance Soviet power and prevent Japanese rearmament. At the time of Richard Nixon's second visit to China (February, 1976), she encouraged U.S. forces to remain in Japan, South Korea, the Philippines, and Thailand in reduced capacity. Despite the death of Chou En-lai (January, 1976), who had piloted China's foreign policy toward the United States, she kept to this course. Stalemate resulted, however, when American public opinion forced Washington to delay implementation of Peking's three demands for "normalization" (full diplomatic recognition): troop withdrawal, severance of relations, and abrogation of the 1954 treaty with Taiwan. Thus, once again U.S.-Chinese *détente* encountered its principal obstacle.

China's relations with Japan improved very slowly because of their conflicting policies toward the United States after 1949. The American-Japanese Security Treaty of 1952, which provided for the presence of American troops in Japan, combined with Chinese fears of renewed "Japanese militarism" to prevent a final peace treaty. In the late 1950s some commerce opened between China and Japan, equal to barely four percent of Japan's trade. Japanese economic expansion into Southeast Asia — commerce, factory re-location, and some foreign aid — disturbed the Chinese, whose Marxist views interpreted this as preparation for imperialist conquest. Indeed, Japan's "economic miracle" of the 1960s appeared to China as a capitalist "Great Leap Forward" into that area.

Still, both powers desired more contacts — China to procure Japanese technology, Japan to obtain coal, iron, and oil from northeastern China. Yet, because of American considerations, neither could act unilaterally. When the United States requested Chinese assistance to evacuate Vietnam, a breakthrough occurred. The new U.S.-China policy permitted Japanese recognition of the People's Republic in September, 1972. Over the next three years commerce between the two nations tripled. China then enticed Japan with the prospect of lucrative oil exploration off the Chinese east coast. A proposed final peace treaty, however, stumbled over Japan's objection to an "anti-hegemony" clause that seemed aimed too obviously at the Soviet Union. Japan desisted, lest she be drawn into the quarrel between the two powers. Hence, Chinese-Japanese accommodation proceeded slowly.

Sino-Russian relations since 1949 have stormed from revolutionary partnership to outright hostility. Mao's policy of "lean to one side" resulted in the alliance treaty of February, 1950, but the conclusion of the Korean War intensified their differences. Truthfully, both countries had little more than ideology and common enemies to unite them. The

Communist Chinese considered Soviet Premier Khrushchev's denunciation of Stalin's "cult of personality" in 1956 an indirect attack on Mao, provoking the Sino-Soviet split. A number of factors fed the conflict: the historical experience from which the Russians recalled the Mongol invasions during the thirteenth through the seventeenth centuries, while the Chinese remembered the perennial barbarian threat on China's northern frontiers, capped by nineteenth-century Czarist imperialism; the territorial issue, in which China demanded that Russia admit the illegality of her occupation of the trans-Amur region, the Maritime Province, Outer Mongolia, and part of Chinese Turkestan, forced from the Manchus after the Opium Wars; the doctrinal dispute, emerging from the late 1920s, when Stalin regarded the proletariat as the "vanguard of revolution," while Mao favored the peasantry; the struggle for hegemony within the Communist family, wherein China claimed leadership of the Third World (or underdeveloped nations) — the historic Middle Kingdom updated — while rejecting the U.S.S.R. as a "social imperialist" and asserting Mao's superiority over contemporary Russian leaders, fully equal to Marx and Lenin as a founding father of Communism; and the debate over strategy and the pace of revolution, which became evident in the late 1950s. China wanted to move rapidly — even to risk atomic war — calculating that her agricultural society could salvage more from that conflict than urban-centered America or the Soviet Union. Russia preferred a more devious route, utilizing infiltration and temporary accommodation with the West. Such divergence of views stemmed largely from differing environmental factors in addition to the generation gap of the two revolutions.

Border clashes occurred in the 1960s along China's northern and western frontiers. During the Cultural Revolution, the Soviets mobilized their huge army along the boundaries of Mongolia and Manchuria. Recalling the thrust of Russian troops into China on three occasions since 1900 (during the Boxer Rebellion, the Northern Campaign, and World War II), the Chinese dug air raid shelters, stockpiled arms, and developed the atomic bomb (October, 1964), and trained the masses in hand-to-hand combat. Faced with Russia's overwhelming military assistance to North Vietnam and naval domination of the Indian Ocean, the Soviet-Indian treaty of 1969, and finally Soviet-Japanese economic cooperation, China struggled to avert containment. The danger of a "surgical strike" by the Soviet army against Sinkiang nuclear installations reached a climax in the spring of that year in an actual clash over an island in the Ussuri River. Mao Tse-tung's death in September, 1976, failed to improve relations despite the efforts of Moscow's special emissary. A year later, restored First Vice-Premier Teng Hsiao-ping announced that China would not renew the old Soviet alliance treaty at its expiration in February, 1980. Thus, the split widened further.

### • The Post-GPCR Period (1969-Present)

Much has changed in China in the years since the end of the Cultural. Revolution in 1969, yet much has remained the same. Like all other revolutions, this one has engendered raucously vitriolic debates both within and outside the country concerning its consequences and achievements in particular. One would not be simplistic to suggest that the Cultural Revolution has dominated Chinese thinking almost as much since 1969 as it did while its fury raged. For the radicals (the very people who sponsored the GPCR and were its prime beneficiaries), there has been overriding concern to argue its necessity, defend its values, and emphasize its positive legacy. For many others, some of whom suffered immensely from its onslaughts, the phenomenon was irrational and reckless, and its proponents foolhardy for having ravaged the nation's political and economic well-being.

The meeting of the Ninth Congress of the CCP in April, 1969, marked the conclusion of the Cultural Revolution and the seeming culmination of Mao's struggle with his opponents. But the coalition of factions which controlled the ruling organs of party, state, and army were hardly of one mind, even without the visible presence of anti-Maoists. As reconstruction and consolidation became primary goals in the immediate aftermath of the GPCR, Chou En-lai began to play an increasingly prominent role in managing affairs of state, all the more so as Mao once again withdrew from public life and Lin Piao (his heir apparent) was killed in a plane crash (September, 1971) while trying to flee China after plotting a coup against Mao. Factional relationships in the early 1970s are especially intricate and resistant to easy analysis on the part of outsiders. Despite this, it has become clear that already in this period moderate and pragmatic elements were beginning to return to positions of influence, including such a major purge victim as Teng Hsiao-ping in early 1973. The rehabilitation of men only recently declared to be "traitors," "capitalist-roaders," and "revisionists" was a major sign that once again the political pendulum in China was swinging in a new direction. By the mid-point of this decade, moderates had filled enough positions to significantly challenge GPCR influence in every area of Chinese life.

In his semi-retirement, Mao was not unaware of what was happening. Working to resist this latest phase of an old problem (the wane of revolutionary fervor, bureaucratism, capitalist backsliding, careerism, and other evils), the Maoists launched at least two major campaigns: the "anti-Lin, anti-Confucius" campaign of 1973-1974, and the "beat back the right deviationist wind" campaign of late 1975. The first had little success

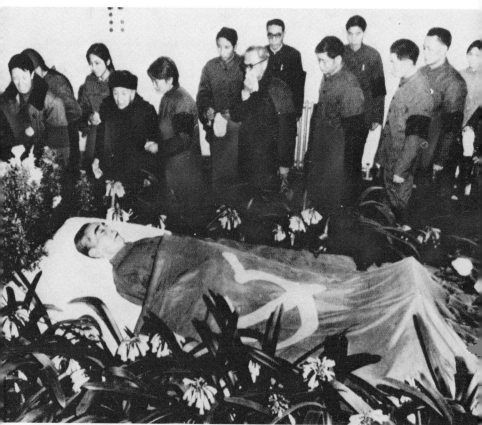

Mourners file past the flag-draped body of Chou En-lai, Premier of the People's Republic of China, at the time of his death in January, 1976. Wide World Photos.

either in arousing much political support or in achieving its goal of forcing the pragmatists to retreat. The second was moderately successful in that it led to the withdrawal from public view and ultimate dismissal from his posts of Teng Hsiao-ping just after the death of Chou En-lai in early January, 1976. Teng's second departure from the inner circle of Chinese leaders and the naming of Hua Kuo-feng as Premier seemed to bode well for the radicals. But since the death of Mao on September 9, 1976, Hua has shown his true colors as a moderate and has used his position to suppress the radicals by arresting their most prominent leaders (collectively known as the "Gang of Four"): Chiang Ch'ing (Mao's wife), Yao Wen-yüan, Wang Hung-wen, and Chang Ch'un-ch'iao. Since July, 1977,

Teng Hsiao-ping has again been rehabilitated and restored to his former position. A new moderate triumvirate, with Hua now as Chairman, Teng returned as Vice Premier, and Yeh Chien-ying, the new Defense Minister, governs China with the backing of the military. At this point, the radicals appear to have lost all influence in Chinese politics. If the history of factionalism is any guide, there may still be a future for radical opinion in the People's Republic. It does seem, however, that with Mao's passing the main strength and heart of that opinion are gone forever. Without his prestige and personal popularity, the radicals may be a doomed species. One may suspect, with certain justification, that China will now proceed slowly along the path pioneered by the Soviet Union, and her leaders will seek to modernize the country through bureaucratic means and will even further institutionalize the dictatorship of the Communist Party. Whether this will be to the advantage of the Chinese people themselves remains to be seen, as the Fifth National People's Congress in early 1978 announced a new constitution and a "Long March" toward making China a superpower.

## Suggestions for Further Reading

Barnett, A. Doak, *China on the Eve of the Communist Takeover* (1963)

Bianco, Lucien, *Origins of the Chinese Revolution, 1915-1949* (1971)

Bodde, Derk, *China's Cultural Tradition* (1957)

Chesneaux, Jean, *Peasant Revolts in China, 1840-1949* (1973)

Chow, Tse-tsung, *The May Fourth Movement: Intellectual Revolution in Modern China* (1960)

Creel, Herrlee G., *Chinese Thought from Confucius to Mao Tse-tung* (1953)

DeBary, William T., et al. (eds.), *Sources of Chinese Tradition* (1960)

Fairbank, John K., (ed.), *The Chinese World Order* (1968)

_____, *The United States and China* (Third edition, 1971)

Fay, Peter Ward, *The Opium War, 1840-1842* (1975)

Gasster, Michael, *China's Struggle to Modernize* (1972)

Hsiao, Kung-ch'uan, *Rural China: Imperial Control in the Nineteenth Century* (1960)

Hsü, Immanuel C. Y., *The Rise of Modern China* (1975)

Hucker, Charles O., *China's Imperial Past* (1975)

Kuhn, Phillip A., *Rebellion and Its Enemies in Late Imperial China* (1970)

Levenson, Joseph R., *Confucian China and Its Modern Fate* (1968)

Leys, Simon, *Chinese Shadows* (1977)

Meskill, John T., *An Introduction to Chinese Civilization* (1973)

Mote, Frederick W., *Intellectual Foundations of China* (1971)

Needham, Joseph, *Science and Civilization in China* (1954)

Schram, Stuart R., *Mao Tse-tung* (1966)

Schurmann, Herbert Franz, *Ideology and Organization in Communist China* (1968)

Sheridan, James E., *China in Disintegration* (1975)

————, *Chinese Warlord: The Career of Feng Yü-hsiang* (1966)

Sih, Paul K. T., *Nationalist China During the Sino-Japanese War, 1937-1945* (1977)

————, *The Strenuous Decade, 1927-1937* (1974)

Snow, Edgar, *Red Star Over China* (1938)

Spence, Jonathan D., *Emperor of China: Self-Portrait of K'ang-hsi* (1974)

Teng, Ssu-yu, and Fairbank, John K., *China's Response to the West* (1954)

Townsend, J., *Politics in China* (1974)

Wakeman, Frederic, Jr., *The Fall of Imperial China* (1975)

Watson, W., *Early Civilization in China* (1966)

Wright, Mary C., (ed.), *China in Revolution: The First Phase, 1900-1913* (1968)

————, *The Last Stand of Chinese Conservatism* (1966)

# *Glossary*

*Analects* — Collection of "sayings" attributed to Confucius.

*Chiang Kai-shek* — Chinese Nationalist leader, successor to Sun Yat-sen after 1925. Movement defeated on the mainland and driven to island of Taiwan in 1949. President of the Republic of China there until his death in 1975.

*Chou En-lai* — Long a party associate of Mao Tse-tung. Premier of the People's Republic from 1949 to his death in 1976. Foreign Minister, 1949-1959.

*chün-tzu* — "Gentleman." The properly-cultivated person; the ideal of Confucianists.

*Confucius* — The "Great Sage" (551-479 B.C.). Philosopher and teacher whose ideals gave China its fundamental character.

*Eight-Legged Essay* — Rigid format for the civil service examinations. Developed during the Ming Dynasty (1368-1644).

*Great Leap Forward* — Campaign launched late in 1957 to raise rapidly China's economic production and create a new society. A significant failure for Mao.

*Great Proletarian Cultural Revolution (GPCR)* — Campaign by Mao Tse-tung (1966-1969) against the moderate policies of Communist-Party pragmatists and the values and attitudes of traditional China.

*Hundred Schools of Thought* — General name for the extraordinary flowering of philosophy along with political and social thought during the Eastern Chou period (771-256 B.C.).

*Jen* — Confucian virtue encompassing benevolence, love, compassion, and sympathy toward one's fellow men.

*Khrushchev, Nikita S.* — Soviet premier whose policies of "de-Stalinization" and "co-existence" with the West were regarded as dangerously "revisionist" by Mao Tse-tung. Vital issues in the Sino-Soviet split after 1956.

*Kuomintang* — The official ruling party of the Republic of China (presently on Taiwan), the KMT. Also known as the Chinese Nationalist Party. Originally founded in 1905 by Sun Yat-sen, who established the Chinese republic following the anti-Manchu revolution (1911-1912).

*Lao Tzu* — Purported author (604?-531 B.C.) of the *Tao-te Ching* and founder of Taoism.

*li* — Confucian virtue denoting social and moral propriety.

*Long March* — The trek of some one hundred thousand supporters of the Chinese Communist Party to escape the forces of Chiang Kai-shek in 1934-1935. Covered five thousand miles from southeastern to northern China. Confirmed Mao Tse-tung's leadership.

*Mandate of Heaven* — Ancient political concept which claims that dynasties come to power with Heaven's consent and remain as long as they provide proper leadership through moral example. If not, the people may rise in revolt.

*Mao Tse-tung* — Undisputed leader of the Chinese Communist Party after 1934-1935. Concept of guerrilla warfare and mobilization of the peasantry captured the countryside of China for the Communists against the Nationalists by 1949. Then Chairman of the Central People's Administrative Council of the People's Republic of China.

*Marshall Mission* — Unsuccessful attempt by the American General George C. Marshall to mediate a peace between the Chinese Communists and the Nationalists from 1945-1947. Its failure resulted in a steady erosion of American support to Chiang Kai-shek from that point.

*mass line* — Technique developed by the Chinese Communist Party during the Yenan Period (1935-1947) to facilitate mass mobilization by providing a link between the party and the masses.

*May Fourth Movement* — A cultural and political campaign launched by Chinese students and intellectuals on May 4, 1919, first precipitated by the resentment against the weak warlord government in Peking as well as the cession of the Shantung concessions to Japan by the Versailles Conference. Subsequently evolved into a modern literary revolutionary movement.

*Middle Kingdom* — *Chung-kuo* or "right in the middle." China perceived as the center of the universe with outside barbarians in a tributary status. The supreme concept of Chinese cultural superiority.

*Pao-chia* — Mechanism for local control through neighborhood self-policing. Inaugurated during the Sung dynasty (960-1279).

*Sino-Soviet split* — Dispute between the Soviet Union and the People's Repbulic of China, emanating from Premier Khrushchev's denunciation of Stalin's "cult of personality" in 1956. Quarrel raged over historical, doctrinal, territorial, hegemonic, and strategic issues.

*Tael* — Chinese coin valued at approximately U.S. $1.63 in the early nineteenth century; at least half of that by 1900.

*Tao* — "The Way" or path to personal and societal happiness and harmony. Each of China's great philosophies offered its own *Tao.*

*Tao-te Ching* — Basic text of Taoist teaching.

*t'i/yung* — "Substance/Function:" from the slogan "Chinese learning for substance, Western learning for function." The approach to reform characteristic of the self-strengtheners of the late nineteenth century.

*tributary system* — Traditional Chinese systematic approach to dealing with barbarians based on the tradition of the Middle Kingdom. China was the center of all things, the foundation of culture, to which non-Chinese brought tribute in return for protection from the emperor and access, through trade, to the immense wealth of China. A familial concept, founded on Confucian principles. Originated by the Han, it reached its zenith in the period of the T'ang (618-906).

*wang* — "king." Title originally reserved for Chou rulers, but increasingly used by feudal lords during the Eastern Chou period (771-256 B.C.)

*well-field system* — Utopian system of land distribution and agricultural practice whereby eight families shared nine equal plots: one for each family's needs, and one worked communally for the local lord, or to pay taxes.

*yin-yang* — A unique Chinese cosmological theory based on two contending, complementary, and interacting cosmic forces governing the universe and its dynamics. *Yang* is the masculine, positive, and active element, while *yin* is the feminine, negative, and passive.

# *Index*